Charles Warren Stoddard

The wonder-worker of Padua

Charles Warren Stoddard
The wonder-worker of Padua
ISBN/EAN: 9783743464957
Manufactured in Europe, USA, Canada, Australia, Japa
Cover: Foto ©ninafisch / pixelio.de

Manufactured and distributed by brebook publishing software (www.brebook.com)

Charles Warren Stoddard

The wonder-worker of Padua

The Wonder-Worker of Padua.

BY THE SAME AUTHOR.

POEMS. Out of Print.

SOUTH SEA IDYLS. Charles Scribner's Sons.

MASHALLA: A Flight into Egypt. D. Appleton & Co.

HAWAIIAN LIFE.—Lazy Letters from Low Latitudes. F. T. Neely.

A TROUBLED HEART. Ave Maria.

THE LEPERS OF MOLOKAI. Ave Maria.

To the
C. W. S. R. C., Salem, Mass.,
With Aloha.

Digitized by the Internet Archive
in 2016 with funding from
Boston Public Library

https://archive.org/details/wonderworkerofpa00stod

The Wonder-Worker of Padua.

PROLOGUE.—THE FIVE FRIARS.

THE afternoon shadows were lengthening under the walls of the monastery of Santa Cruz, a house of the Canons Regular of St. Augustine, at Coimbra. Life within that holy house stole on as slowly, as regularly, and for the most part as silently, as those deepening shadows. Each morning it was renewed as cheerfully as broke the dawn upon the waves that wash the shores of Portugal; each noon it was radiant with the fulness of spiritual joy; each evening it hushed itself to rest with prayer and praise; and these three epochs in the daily life of the cloister were heralded by the mellow peal of the Angelus as it was wafted over the embosoming hills, and throbbed into silence in far-off, fainting echoes.

Now and again something occurred in the monastery—something slight in itself, but enough to break in upon the peaceful current of events and create an interest or excitement that fairly startled the gentle occupants. There were guests from time to time—quite a number of them; for the worldly are ever curious concerning the inner life of those who though in the world are not of it. Therefore there was a guest-master at Santa Cruz, as there is always a guest-master in every monastery; and his office it is to receive those who desire to see the chapels, the relics, the cloisters. It is the duty and the pleasure of this guest-master to conduct visitors through the monastery and to entertain them; and thus relieve the friars from all distractions, such as sudden and unexpected calls from prayer or labor.

One day at Santa Cruz five stranger guests arrived—three priests and two lay-brothers, disciples of St. Francis, whose Order was then but ten years old. These friars had been assigned to the mission in Morocco, and were on their way thither when they sought the hospitality of the Abbey of Santa Cruz. Who shall say that it was chance alone that brought them thither? They were Franciscans. Not far distant from Coimbra, the pious Queen of Portugal had established the Convent of St. Anthony of Olivares; it was situated in an olive grove, whence it derived its name. The house was small and poor, but it was large enough to shelter the five friars; and the Brother Questor, whose duty it was to ask alms for the needs of the brethren, would have gladly shared his frugal fare with these apostles who were on their way to martyrdom in Morocco. But they passed Olivares and sought the gates of Santa

Cruz, and were there given heartfelt welcome.

Was it for this reason that, as the Franciscan chronicles tell us, "Queen Urraca sent for and lovingly received the friars"? For indeed she had their Order in great esteem, and inquired many things concerning their errand, most courteously offering to supply all their wants. Not content with the brief account of their General's intention which they gave her, this lady, thirsting as the hart for the word of God, engaged them in spiritual discourse, drawing thence much sweetness and consolation; then, taking them apart, she besought them, for the love of Him for whose sweet name they were going to torments and death, to beg of Almighty God to reveal to them the day on which she should die. And, albeit the friars endeavored by all means to escape her importunity, saying that they were most unworthy to know the secrets of the Lord, and other words of like import, yet did she at length prevail with them to give her that promise which she craved. And so, after fervent prayer, they again came before the Queen and bade her be of good courage; for that it was the will of God that her end should be very shortly, and before that of the King, her husband. Moreover, they gave her a sure sign; for, "Know, lady," they said, "that before many days we shall die by the sword for the faith of Christ. Praised be His Divine Majesty, who has chosen us, poor men, to be in the number of His martyrs! Our bodies shall be brought into this city with great devotion by the Christians of Morocco, and you and your husband shall go to meet them. When these things shall come to pass, know that the time is come for you to leave this world and go to God."

The guest-master of Santa Cruz was a youth of four and twenty, who was already ordained. He had a marvellously beautiful countenance and was singularly engaging in manner. Naturally, he was thrown much in the society of the friars, and often conversed with them of the extraordinary history of Portiuncula and of the miracles wrought by their seraphic Father, St. Francis of Assisi. Certain it is that the five friars perished in their blood at the hands of the infidels. Their bodies were brought home in solemn state, attended by various supernatural manifestations calculated to inspire reverence and awe.

It was the King's wish that these relics of the first Franciscan martyrs should rest in the principal church of the capital; but they were mysteriously guided or conveyed to the monastery of Santa Cruz, where they had lodged, and where his Majesty had a superb chapel erected, in which the relics were reposited.

Many marvels were witnessed at that

shrine, and these deeply touched the heart and the spirit of the young guest-master. But a few months before he had held converse with these very friars, who were then joyously seeking the palm and the crown of martyrdom; now they were in paradise, and he was kneeling beside their holy dust,—a poor friar groping blindly after that light that should illumine him and make clear his path of life.

One day, kneeling at that tomb, his heart aflame with love and veneration, from the depths of his soul he cried out: "O that the Most High would grant me to be associated with them in their glorious sufferings! That to me also it were given to be persecuted for the faith—to bare my neck to the executioners! Will that blessed day ever dawn for thee, Fernando? Will such happiness ever be thine?" Thus, through chaste communion with the five friars—call it not chance that brought their hearts together, — through the sufferings, by the sacrifice, and at the tomb of the five martyrs, did Fernando de Bouillon find his vocation.

I.—FERNANDO THE NOVICE.

Who was Fernando de Bouillon? He was the son of Martino de Bouillon, and Teresa Tavera, his wife, who were of ancient lineage and noble birth. Don Martino descended from the illustrious Godfrey de Bouillon, who led the first Crusade and was the first Frankish King of Jerusalem. He was the grandson of Vincenzo de Bouillon, who followed King Alfonzo I. in his campaign against the Moors, and who, in acknowledgment of his deeds of valor, was made governor of Lisbon. This office became hereditary in the family of De Bouillon; and Fernando, as first son of the house, was heir to it. And Doña Teresa was hardly less illustrious. Her ancestors had reigned over the Asturias in the eighth century, until the invasion by the Saracens.

Don Martino and Doña Teresa occupied a sumptuous palace close to the cathedral of Lisbon. Here Fernando was born on the 15th of August, 1195. Eight days after his birth he was carried with great pomp to the cathedral, and there received in baptism the name of Fernando.

Though nothing of a prophetic nature preceded the birth of Fernando, it was soon evident that he was no ordinary child. Born on the Feast of the Assumption, it was at the shrine of Our Lady del' Pilar he received the grace of baptism. To the Blessed Virgin his mother consecrated the babe when returning from the baptismal font; Maria was the first name he learned to utter, and the hymn he heard oftenest from his mother's lips was "O Gloriosa Domina!" As a child, the sight of an image or a painting of the Madonna would change his tears to smiles; as a religious, he placed himself under the special protection of the Blessed Virgin; as an apostle, he was her champion, ever sounding her praises, ever ready to do battle in her cause. At the age of ten, beautiful in form and feature, with an inner spiritual beauty that gave his face an almost angelic expression, possessed of a sweet and gladsome nature, a quick intelligence and a lively imagination, he had already shown a preference for the secluded paths of a religious life.

During five hears of his infancy Fernando attended the cathedral school in Lisbon, clothed in the garb of a cleric. He was a pattern of all the proprieties. In this exquisitely refined child virtue blossomed like a flower, and breathed forth a delicate fragrance that all who approached him became conscious of.

It was now he gave the first manifestation of that power which, through him, was to work wonders so long as he lived,—

wonders that have never ceased, and are never to cease in this ever-wondering world. Kneeling one day at the shrine of Our Lady in the cathedral, his eyes on the tabernacle wherein the Blessed Sacrament was veiled, a demon, one of those baleful spirits that still tempt and delude the unwary, appeared before him. Startled as he was, with the pious instinct of nature he traced upon the marble step where he was kneeling the Sign of the Cross. The vision vanished, but to this hour is seen that sacred symbol indelibly impressed upon the marble. In that hour Fernando's fate was sealed.

With everything to make life alluring—youth, beauty, health, wealth, high birth and gentle breeding, devoted parents and idolizing friends,—the child turned from them all. It was his destiny. Already able to meditate upon the foolish rewards of life and labors in the world and for the world alone, Fernando exclaimed: "O world, how burthensome thou art become! Thy power is but that of a fragile reed; thy riches are as a puff of smoke, and thy pleasures like a treacherous rock whereon virtue is shipwrecked."

He seems to have resolved on this occasion to enter the religious life; to turn from the luxurious delights that had never appealed to his nature, and accept poverty, humility, and obedience as his portion. This resolution once formed, nothing could cause him to reconsider it.

At the gate of the Abbey of St. Vincent he implored admission; "being attracted thither," as the chronicle quaintly records, "by the renown for learning and holiness of its men." Surely nothing could have offered him a more pleasing prospect than the society of such as these; nothing afforded him more perfect satisfaction.

II.—FERNANDO THE SCHOLASTIC.

What wonder that the child should have turned from the world in his fifteenth year, when most children at that stage of development find an indescribable joy in mere physical existence? From his earliest infancy his life was an involuntary consecration. He was meekness, compassion, love personified. He had a special devotion to the impoverished and all those in sorrow and affliction. He was never known to utter a falsehood. All the offices of the Church were dear to him. He never failed to hear Mass daily, and joyfully and most reverently to serve. Our Blessed Lady, pattern of purity, was his chosen patroness. For the amusements which were the delight of his companions he cared nothing; the pleasures of life he never knew, and hoped never to know. He was the natural enemy of idleness; was instinctively studious; and of a sweet solemnity, which did not oppress but rather edified his associates, and endeared him to them.

What wonder that he should turn from the madding crowd and seek the seclusion of a cloister? There was nothing unwholesome, nothing unnatural in his resolve to quit the world while yet a child in years. For a youth of his temperament—a temperament which was an angelic heritage—there is really but one step to be taken; firmly, but in all humility, he took it.

Without the walls of Lisbon stood the Monastery of St. Vincent, a house of the Canons Regular of St. Augustine. Having obtained the leave of his parents, he went thither; and, casting himself at the feet of the prior—called by some Gonsalvo Mendez and by others Pelagius,—he asked to be admitted to the holy brotherhood. Naturally edified by the gentle and reverent spirit of the youth who knelt before him, the prior received him with affectionate tenderness, and in due course of time he was clothed in the white robe of the Order.

What happiness of heart was his, what peace of spirit, what serenity of soul! Alas! they were short-lived. His friends, missing him sorely, sought him at all seasons. If he had before this been to them an engaging mystery, a surprise by reason of his unlikeness to them and to any other whom they knew, he was now, clad in the pale robe of the Augustinians, their wonder and delight. He drew them irresistibly to the monastery, and their well-meant but ill-timed visitations were a distraction which he could not long endure.

Two years were enough, and more than enough, to assure him that at St. Vincent's, let him strive never so bravely against such a fate, he was in danger of losing his vocation. He must seek security in solitude, in exile; and that without delay, if he would attain the perfection which was his aim in life. It was in no bitterness of spirit, no pride, no impatience, he turned from all who loved him most. It was an honest and an earnest effort on his part to reach that state of grace for which his heart was hungering night and day. At St. Vincent's he was neighbor to the world and the worldly life he cared not for. He must fly hence, at any cost to comfort, temporal or spiritual. He must steel his heart to the sweet assaults of earthly love; for the unity, peace and concord he sought found no abiding place under heaven save in cloistral seclusion.

The prior of St. Vincent's had, during the two years of Fernando's sojourn there, beheld with joy the fervor of the youth; and when that youth implored him to be allowed to depart into some other house of the Order—some house far removed from

Lisbon and the voices that were constantly crying to him to return to them again,—the prior was for a season loath to give him leave; but, as the old chronicler says: "Having at length, by tears and prayers, obtained the consent of his superior, he quitted not the army in which he was enlisted, but the scene of combat; not through caprice, but in a transport of fervor."

III.—FERNANDO THE AUGUSTINIAN CANON.

Nearly a hundred miles from Lisbon stood the Abbey of Santa Cruz. It was lapped in the seclusion of Coimbra; it was far from the trials, the temptations, the tribulations of the work-a-day world. It was the mother-house of the Augustinians, the head cradle of the Order. The sweet influences of the saintly Theaton, its first prior, still perfumed it. It was the centre and the source of all the noblest traditions of the tribe, the inspiration of the clergy, the consolation and the pride of the loyal and widely scattered brotherhood.

The Abbey was a far-famed seat of learning. There Religion and Letters went hand in hand. Don John and Don Raymond, both Doctors of the University of Paris, were among the scholars at Santa Cruz. For a student, for a religious, for a recluse, there was no retreat in Portugal more desirable than this; and thither Fernando was sent.

His new brethren were not long in convincing themselves that Fernando's change of residence had not been made without reflection, and that the love of novelty had no share in his decision. He had, it is true, ardently longed for solitude and tranquillity; but, far from seeking therein a dispensation from the rigor of monastic life, he sought but a means to perfect himself in virtue. At Lisbon he had read the literature of pagan antiquity; at Santa Cruz he devoted himself to the study of theology, the Fathers, history, religious controversy. Above all these, the Sacred Scriptures won his ardent attention.

He was seventeen years of age when he entered Santa Cruz. He was completely detached from the world. Nature had in every way richly endowed him. His memory was prodigious. All knowledge came to him freely, without effort; and, once acquired, it never left him more, but, beautifully adjusted and ready for instant use, it seemed literally at his tongue's end.

Eight years he passed at Santa Cruz, in obedience, in prayer, in study. He grew continually in virtue—he was virtue's self. Devoted to his books, he never permitted the study of them to interfere with the pious duties allotted him. On one occasion, being employed in some remote part of the Abbey, he heard the note of the Elevation bell; turning toward the chapel, he prostrated himself, and beheld the distant altar, and the Sacred Host in the hands of the celebrant,—beheld them all as plainly as if the intervening walls had vanished away.

Nor was this the only wonder he worked at Santa Cruz. While nursing one of the religious, the patient—a victim of obsession—became uncontrollable. Fernando, spreading the hem of his mantle over the sufferer, brought to him instant and permanent relief.

His erudition grew to be the subject of general comment. He knew the Holy Bible by heart; he seemed to have taken the sense and substance of it to his soul, so that it became a part of him. In one of his commentaries he wrote: "O divine Word, admirable Word, that inebriatest and changest the heart, Thou art the limpid source that refreshest the parched soul; the ray of hope that givest comfort to the poor sinner; the faithful messenger that bringest glad tidings to us exiles of our heavenly country!"

He never forgot what he had once studied; though the time was to come when the calls upon him were so many and so various he had no moment in which to read anything save only his breviary.

IV.—FERNANDO BECOMES ANTONIO.

Not far from the Monastery of Santa Cruz, at Olivares, stood the Franciscan Abbey of the Olives. This holy house was small and poor. It was named in honor of St. Anthony of the Desert; his poverty, his frugality, his sobriety were patterns for the *frati* who dwelt there. They lived upon the tribute gathered by the humble supplicants who went forth daily asking alms of the faithful. Often they had knocked at Fernando's door; often he had shared his bread and his wine with them; and he was beginning to feel a personal interest in them when the five friars who were afterward martyred in Morocco sought the hospitality of Santa Cruz, where he soon grew to know them intimately.

The martyrdom of the friars, the transportation of their relics to Portugal, and the shrine prepared for them at Santa Cruz, the knowledge he had gained of the origin and development of the Franciscan Order, inspired Fernando with a longing to become himself a follower of St. Francis.

Now the solitude he had sought and found in the cloister at Santa Cruz began to pale. He feared he was wasting his life; he felt that his energy and enthusiasm should be placed at the disposal of those who were in crying need; and surely there were many such. He would even follow in the footsteps of the five friars; he also would offer his body to be martyred for Christ's sake and for love of his fellowmen. Therefore when the Brother Questor, whose duty it was to ask alms for the needs of the Convent at Olivares, came to Santa Cruz, Fernando talked long and earnestly with him concerning the rule of his Order and the wonderful founder thereof.

This Brother Questor and Fernando were

in close sympathy. One day when Fernando was saying Mass the Brother Questor died. At that moment Fernando, dissolved in ecstasy, saw his soul in its flight through purgatory, ascending dove-like into the realms of bliss. It may have been this vision, or it may have been the glorious sacrifice of the martyr friars, or the poverty and devotion of the brotherhood, that inspired Fernando with the desire to become one of them; we know not what was the primal cause, but we know that with difficulty he obtained leave of the prior of Santa Cruz to detach himself from the Augustinians and join the followers of St. Francis.

He had won the respect, the love, the esteem, the admiration of his associates at Santa Cruz; they would fain not part with him. One said to him, half in jest and half in earnest: "Go thy way; thou wilt surely become a saint." Fernando replied: "When they tell thee I am a saint, then bless thou the Lord.''

In applying for admission to the Franciscan ranks, Fernando had said: "With all the ardor of my soul do I desire to take the holy habit of your Order; and I am ready to do so upon one condition—that, after clothing me with the garb of penance, you send me to the Saracens, so that I also may deserve to participate in the crown of your holy martyrs."

Then he put off the white robe of the Augustinians and donned the brown garb of the impoverished Franciscans; took unto himself the name of Antonio, the patron of the hermitage of Olivares; and, without one adieu, joyfully vanished from the knowledge of all those who had known and loved him in the flesh.

V.—ANTHONY SEEKS MARTYRDOM.

Not all who seek shall find. Antonio, or Anthony, was permitted to go to Morocco, where he hoped to end his days in an effort toward the conversion of the Moslems. What dreams were his! what hopes, what aspirations! He was now in very truth following in the footsteps of the five friars who were his first inspiration. He was in a land whose history was made glorious by Tertullian, St. Augustine, St. Fulgentius; great pontiffs and learned doctors. The day of its prosperity was over and gone. Its flourishing churches had fallen to decay, and the arrogance of the infidel made it unsafe for a Christian to pace the narrow streets of those white-walled cities unattended.

Under an ever-cloudless sky, in the glare of the fierce sunshine and the heat of the desert dust, Anthony was stricken down with fever. Filippo of Spain, a young lay-brother who had attached himself to his person, watched with Anthony the whole winter. Not once did the would-be martyr have the opportunity of exposing himself to the fury of the African fanatics. He was utterly prostrated; his life seemed to be slowly ebbing away. Evidently his efforts as a missioner in Morocco were doomed. The fact could not be kept a secret; and accordingly Anthony and Filippo were recalled to Portugal by their superiors, after an absence of but four months.

They dutifully embarked, though their hearts were heavy with disappointment. The martyr's palm might wither in the desert; it was evidently not reserved for them. Neither were they destined to return to Portugal. A white squall struck their vessel, and it was cast upon the Sicilian shore. Anthony and Filippo landed at

Taormina, and at once made their way to Messina, where there was a convent of the Friars Minor. Here for two months the young friars reposed; here health and strength returned to Anthony, and he entered upon a new lease of life. Here, in the convent garden, he planted a lemon tree that flourishes to this hour; for, like the orange tree planted by St. Dominic at Santa Sabina on the Aventine, time can not wither it; and every succeeding year bud, blossom and fruit give testimony of its eternal youth.

About this time the official notice of the convocation of the fourth general chapter of the Franciscan Order reached Messina. Anthony, Filippo, and certain of the Sicilian friars resolved to go to Assisi; and it was Anthony's desire to place himself at the disposal of the holy founder. In doing the will of St. Francis he felt that he could make no error; and that it was the providence of God alone that had recalled him from Africa, shipwrecked him upon the Sicilian coast, and was now about to bring him into the presence of the seraphic Father whose child he had become.

Having celebrated the Easter festivities at Messina, Anthony, accompanied by Filippo and the Sicilian *frati*, set forth on his pilgrimage to Assisi.

VI.—ANTHONY AND ST. FRANCIS.

The fourth general chapter of the Franciscan Order opened at Portiuncula on May 30, 1221. This chapter was a marvellous manifestation of the influence exercised by St. Francis over his followers. It was an all-powerful influence, and it was ever increasing; time alone was necessary to enable it to expand and spread unto the very ends of the earth.

St. Francis, a year previous, had resigned his office of Minister-General. He had, in a certain sense, completed his mission. His Order was well established, was in the most flourishing condition; recruits were constantly approaching him, and at his feet offering the labor of their lives. His wish was law: no one questioned it. His will was their wisdom, his word was final. This stupendous organization, the inspiration and the accomplishment of one mind, had yet a price to be paid for it, and a high price it proved to be: it was no less than the life of the holy founder.

Hoping to find a little much-needed rest, St. Francis shifted the burden of responsibility upon the shoulders of Peter of Catania; but the death of Peter within the year compelled the enfeebled Francis once more to assume the reins of government. He conferred upon Brother Elias the office of Vicar-General, and thus Brother Elias became the mouthpiece of the founder. He was literally a mouthpiece; for, owing to his physical debility, the voice of the Saint could scarcely be raised above a whisper. The voice of Elias was indeed as the voice of Francis, and was listened to by all in unquestioning silence and obedience.

This is what Anthony beheld as he stood in the multitude assembled at Portiuncula: more than two thousand friars gathered together from every part of Europe. They were presided over by Cardinal Ranerio Capaccio; but St. Francis was the magnet that drew them thither, the power that swayed them as one man, whose burning and sole desire was to do the will of their seraphic Father.

As the fruit of his husbandry, Francis could proudly point to Silvester the contemplative; Giles the ecstatic: Thomas of Celano, the noble singer of the *Stabat Mater;* John of Piana; Carpino, and many another,—all these bearing the marks of suffering, but all brave and steadfast warriors for the faith. Here they were, bowing at the knee of the patriarch, humbly waiting his will. And he, pale and emaciated, sinking under a prostration that threatened to terminate his life at any moment, the patron of humility and zeal and love,— when he, in a faint whisper, proposed a mission to Germany, eighty friars sprang to their feet and shouted with enthusiasm that they were ready to do his will there as anywhere and everywhere.

Unnoticed in this great throng, ravished by the spectacle of the Saint and his disciples, trembling with profound emotion, and faint for the fire of love that was consuming him, stood a youth of six and twenty, who was one day to become the most famous of the followers of St. Francis. Yet not one eye was turned upon him in kindness or in curiosity; not one word was spoken to him: he was utterly unnoticed and ignored.

VII.—ANTHONY DESPISED AND REJECTED.

St. Francis was wont to read the hearts and the consciences of his children,—a gift that must have aided him often in their wise direction. Were it not evidently predestined, it would be surprising that the Saint did not recognize in the youthful Anthony one who was anon to be all in all to him and to his holy Order. There he was, this giant in embryo, in the prime of life, singularly attractive to the eye, of fascinating manners, radiant with divine love, virtuous, valiant, face to face with the one who was most to influence him in life—and he was suffered to pass by unnoticed.

One thought was now uttermost in Anthony's mind. He could not again return to Portugal,—that would seem like a step backward and a sign of failure. He must abide near St. Francis. He felt that he could no longer live happily and holily apart from the seraphic one, who so powerfully influenced all those who were attracted to him. For this reason he offered himself to the Provincials and Guardians of Italy. St. Francis, hearing of this, highly approved of the youth's renunciation of his family, his friends, and his country; and recommended him to those who were in need of an assistant.

His services were declined by all; he was not welcome and not wanted. In a great measure, he was himself the cause of his unsuccess; yet the wisdom or the unwisdom of his motive can no longer be questioned when we take into consideration the natural consequences thereof.

With no affectation of humility, the young friar kept secret all knowledge of his past. He assumed an air that bordered on stupidity. It is hardly surprising that he was looked upon with disapproval by the masters of novices, who were accustomed critically to inspect such candidates as offered themselves from time to time at the novitiate. They did not for a moment suspect that he had talents and learning of no mean order.

He proffered his services as assistant in the kitchen; he volunteered to sweep the house well; he asked nothing more than to be allowed to do this for the love of God. Even here his hopes were for a season thwarted. His slight figure had not yet rounded after the ravages of fever; his face, naturally one of the most beautiful among men, was still drawn and pale. He did not look equal to the calls upon the convent drudge, and was unceremoniously dismissed. His early biographer, John Peckham, observes: "No Provincial thought of asking for him." He was deemed unfit for service of any kind.

His case was beginning to to grow desperate. What could he hope to do for the greater glory of God and the love of his fellowmen? Would no one take pity on him? Would no one give him some duty to perform? In his extremity he drew Father Gratian, the Provincial of Bologna, aside and implored his aid. It chanced that Father Gratian was in need of a priest to say Mass at a small hospice, where six lay-brothers formed the community. "Are you a priest?" asked Father Gratian of the unpromising youth. "I am," replied Anthony.

This seemed like a sad awakening from his dreams of the future. Not Africa, not martyrdom, apparently not Italy, could he claim for his portion; but Father Gratian, who must send a priest to the lay-brothers in their retreat, found him sufficient in an extremity; and thereupon he was ordered away into the mountains to say Mass for the recluses in a very little house hidden in a lonely place.

VIII.—ANTHONY THE CONTEMPLATIVE.

From the very foundation of the Order, the Franciscans have possessed two kinds of holy houses. There were the large convents, usually erected in cities or their suburbs, where the friars diligently attended the many calls upon their time, sympathy and strength; and there were small convents, or hermitages, often hidden away in the fastnesses of the mountains or the forest.

One of these minor houses was situated not far from Forli, upon the slopes of the Apennines. In all Tuscany there was not a more secluded spot. Monte Paolo was an ideal home for Anthony. Separated from the outer world by a far-spreading wood; walled in by rocky heights, where only the birds nested and the wild goat climbed; visited by heaven-sent zephyrs;

nourished by the uncultivated fruits which nature so lavishly contributed; refreshed by a delicious spring of crystal purity,— that sweet solitude seemed indeed to the ill-judged and disappointed friar an earthly paradise.

Here Anthony said Mass daily for the little company of brethren; here he begged leave to assist them in their labors, counting it a privilege so to do. They allotted him his task, and he cheerfully accepted and performed it. They had not yet discovered that he was a man far their superior in all respects; for he became one with them —one with them in spirit and in truth,— but he was the holiest of them all.

Within the grounds of the hermitage at Monte Paolo was secreted a deep grotto; and within the grotto a cell had been hewn out of the rock, and here Anthony found his perfect joy. One of the brethren had long used this cell as a storehouse for his tools, but he willingly surrendered it to Anthony when the latter ventured to ask if he might have the use of it; and there the friar passed most of his time.

Nearly a year Anthony passed in the wilderness. His bed was straw; his pillow a stone; his food and drink a little bread and water. He mortified himself by fasting, took the discipline, and gladly endured other austerities and voluntary pains.

During most of that year, so far as the Rule of the Order and the spirit of obedience permitted, he dwelt alone in his hollow rock. His time he passed in study, meditation, and ever-ardent prayer. He translated the Psalms of David, enriching them with notes and commentaries suitable for the use of preachers. Wittingly or unwittingly, he was preparing himself for a fresh field of labor; and perhaps nowhere else, outside of the desert itself, could he have found so suitable a time and place for just such preparation.

From a cavern came St. Francis, St. Bernard, St. Norbert, and St. Benedict; it was fitting that he who was to become a saint as great, powerful and glorious as these should come also from a cavern. The Hermitage of Monte Paolo has been by old chroniclers compared to the cells of the solitaries of the Thebaid. Not a trace of the building itself remains, and more's the pity! In 1629 Signor Paganelli erected an oratory near the grotto consecrated by the prayers and penances of Anthony, in gratitude for a miraculous recovery from illness obtained through his intercession

Emmanuel Azevedo, one of Anthony's biographers, upon visiting the spot, found, about half-way up the mountain, a limpid spring that was never known to become turbid, even in the time of rains, when all the neighboring springs were thick with mud. He was assured, not only by the peasants whose love for the Saint may have made them too credulous, but by resident priests—it was also the testimony of distinguished travellers,—that on Monte Paolo (better known as St. Anthony's Mountain), during the most violent tempests, when the neighboring heights were swept by furious winds and lashing rains, a calm as of a summer twilight prevailed; and that persons overtaken by the storm hastened to reach the favored spot, knowing full well that there they would be safe from harm—lapped in an atmosphere as serene as the soul of the Saint.

IX.—ANTHONY THE PREACHER.

For a little time only was Anthony permitted to remain in comfortable and peaceful obscurity. Solitude and silence he always loved; but, alas! he was no longer to enjoy them uninterruptedly. In Ember week—March 19, 1222, according to the historian Azzoguidi—the ceremony of ordination called to Forli a number of religious, both Friars Minor and Friar Preachers, who were to receive Holy Orders. Father Gratian and Anthony were also present, but neither in the least suspected the surprise that was in store for all.

Father Gratian, who had not failed to note the edifying fervor of the young priest, as well as the gleams of uncommon intelligence which Anthony was not always able to disguise, was glad to have this opportunity of calling the hermit of Monte Paolo from his vigils to attend the functions at Forli. Father Gratian had been requested by the bishop of the province to deliver to the candidates for ordination the customary address on the sublimity of the priestly office. This honor he courteously offered to the sons of St. Benedict—many of whom were present;—but they, being unprepared, refused to speak on so solemn an occasion. It began to look as if the ceremonies were likely to be interrupted.

Suddenly, as if by intuition, Father Gratian turned to Anthony and desired him to exhort the candidates. The simplicity and beauty of his language and the grace of his manner were greatly in his favor; but he had never yet spoken in public, and since he had become a Friar Minor he had opened no book save only his breviary and the Psalms. Therefore he modestly pleaded his inexperience and his inability; he confessed that he was fitter to serve in the refectory than to preach to the learned who were present. He was covered with confusion, and heartily wished himself back again in his grotto at Monte Paolo. The superior was inflexible; and, rejecting all excuses, he directed Anthony to preach out of obedience, and gave him for a text: "Christ became for us obedient unto death, even the death of the Cross."

The young priest arose, trembling with humility; in a low voice, the beauty of which had been often commented upon, he addressed the Franciscans and Dominicans, who were filled with curiosity and expectation. As he proceeded, his voice gathered volume and his speech fire; his cheek flushed with fervor; his body swayed as a reed in the wind; his wrapped gaze seemed fixed upon a heaven invisible to others, and he spoke as one divinely inspired. His hour of triumph had come at last, unsought and uninvited.

Is it any wonder that all present were astonished beyond measure, and that they looked upon this maiden effort of the novice as little short of miraculous? It is true that his whole life had been a kind of preparation for the pulpit, but an involuntary and unconscious one. His range of experience had been large; every emotion of the heart he had sounded to its depths; in his solitary hours of abstraction he had, in spirit, again and again communed with the martyrs of Morocco and the Canons Regular of Coimbra. He was storm-tossed in the Mediterranean; prostrated upon a bed of pain in Africa; an obscure and unobserved pilgrim at Assisi; an humble servitor and solitary at Monte Paolo.

Now all returned to him like a flash in brilliant and luminous retrospection; and with all else came knowledge — a revival of knowledge,—his knowledge of the Holy Scriptures and of the consecrated writings of the Fathers, together with his own voluminous comments thereon, and a world of wisdom withal,—of wisdom not of this world only.

In a torrent of eloquence that thrilled and amazed his listeners, he developed his discourse with the skill of a logician, the art of an orator, the charm of one predestined to the pulpit; and brought his last period to a conclusion amidst a chorus of enthusiastic approbation. On the instant he found himself conspicuous in a life of publicity,—the life he had sought in vain to fly from. Now, in deed and in very truth, his inner life was ended: he was henceforth to be known as Anthony the Preacher.

X.—ANTHONY THE LECTOR.

The Provincial of Romagna, who was present when Anthony delivered his first sermon, at once appointed the young apostle a preacher in his province; and St. Francis, hearing of the extraordinary effect produced by the sermon, not only confirmed the Provincial's appointment, but greatly enlarged Anthony's sphere of usefulness by giving him leave to preach anywhere and everywhere, whenever an opportunity offered. And yet to preach *only* was not his mission

St. Francis desired that Anthony should apply himself to the study of theology, in order that he might speak with more confidence and authority, and likewise be able to instruct other of his brethren. Neither St. Francis nor any one else was aware of the nature and extent of Anthony's learning;

and he was therefore sent to Vercelli to study theology in the Monastery of St. Andrew, of the Canons Regular, then under the discipline of Abbot Thomas, the greatest living doctor in all Italy. Thomas was one of the Canons Regular whom Mgr. Sessa, Bishop of Vercelli, had called from the Monastery of St. Vincent of Paris to that of St. Andrew of Vercelli, on account of their many virtues and accomplishments.

We may readily imagine the rapid progress so holy a religious as Anthony must have made at St. Andrew's,—he who had already enjoyed the hidden treasures of Heaven. A companion in his studies was Adam de Marisco, of Somerset, diocese of Bath, England; afterward Doctor of the University of Oxford, and finally Bishop of Ely,—a man famous for piety and learning. These young men were received by Abbot Thomas with the utmost tenderness, and in them he found pupils devoted to their studies, of intense application and surpassing intelligence. Anthony was still living under the rule of his Order; for St. Francis had obtained from the Bishop of Vercelli a convent situated near the ancient Church of St. Matthew; and here he dwelt, going at appointed hours to class at St. Andrew's.

Franciscan historians assure us that, though Anthony applied himself most diligently to his studies, he did not fail to preach the Lenten sermons in Milan and other places near at hand; and that on these occasions his lucid exposition of the Scriptures astonished and delighted his hearers. Even in the classroom he was a marvel. One of his teachers says that while explaining to his pupils a work on the "Celestial Hierarchy," Anthony spoke concerning the different orders of celestial spirits with great precision and wonderful intelligence; and it seemed to all who heard him as if he were in the very presence of that hierarchy.

So rapid was Anthony's progress in his studies, so comprehensive his grasp, and so felicitous his treatment of every theme under consideration, that his classmates with one accord urgently begged that he would impart to them something of the knowledge that seemed his birthright. He hesitated; they persistently implored. Anthony knew that the rule of the Order was founded upon poverty, humility, the scorn of all things worldly; and he feared that a show of learning might be considered scandalous rather than edifying. Holiness and humility come first of all; science and the polite accomplishments should follow in their course.

That he might observe to the letter the holy rule and give no cause for scandal, Anthony wrote to St. Francis asking his will in the matter. Now, there is not the shadow of a doubt that St. Francis had the good—the best good—of the Order at heart;

that for this reason he desired gradually to work certain reforms; that he feared a tendency on the part of his followers to an over-interest in the affairs of this life to the neglect of those of the life which is to come. So he wrote to Anthony. The letter has fortunately been preserved in "The Chronicles of the Twenty-Four Generals." It runs as follows:

"To his dear Brother Anthony, Brother Francis sends greeting in the Lord.

"It is my wish that thou teach the brethren sacred theology; yet in such a manner as not to extinguish in thyself and others the spirit of prayer and devotion, according as it is prescribed in the rule.

"The Lord spare thee!

"BROTHER FRANCIS."

Thus was Anthony chosen by the patriarch of Assisi to depart into Bologna and there assume the office of Lector of Theology. Unhappily, no notes of his lectures then and there delivered have been preserved to us; but from his "Commentary on the Psalms" we can judge of the spirit that pervaded them. Because of the nature of this spirit there have been those of his brotherhood who have assured themselves that Anthony was the author of "The Imitation of Christ." The authorship of that inspiring work has long been a vexed question; but Francis Richard Cruise, M. D., in his ingenious and exhaustive work on "Thomas à Kempis,"* seems to have finally settled it.

In his lectures Anthony avoided dry speculation; he brought youthful enthusiasm, coupled with the purest and loftiest mysticism, to bear upon the minds and hearts of his pupils. "To know, to love!" this was his teaching. To know, so that one may love highly and holily; to love, so

---

* London: Kegan Paul, Trench & Co., 1887.

that one may acquire the knowledge that is born of ardor, devotion, self-sacrifice, singleness of purpose—the flower and the fruit of love.

XI.—ATHONY THE FATHER OF MYSTIC THEOLOGY.

St. Francis was the inspirer and St. Bonaventure the most illustrious representative of the mystic school of theology; but Thomas Gallo, Pope Gregory IX., and St. Bonaventure himself, have styled Anthony the father of the school.

Many were the titles conferred upon the inspired gospeller. Cardinal Guy de Montfort, being dangerously ill, was miraculously healed through the intercession of St. Anthony; and he therefore made a pilgrimage to the tomb of the Saint at Padua, and left at that shrine a splendid reliquary, embellished with verses wherein the Saint is hailed as the "star of Spain, pearl of poverty, father of science, model of purity, light of Italy, doctor of divine truth, and glory of Padua."

This father of mystic theology and founder of the mystic school of the Middle Ages was from the very beginning a wonder-worker. His preaching was nearly always confirmed by miracles; the very sermon itself was in some senses miraculous. He must have possessed the gift of tongues. While in Italy he preached in Italian; yet all the knowledge he possessed of that mellifluous tongue he got during his brief intercourse with the six illiterate lay-brothers at the hospice in the solitude of Monte Paolo. While in France he preached in French, though he had never studied the language. Perhaps more remarkable still is the fact that the simple-minded and the most ignorant listeners were capable of fully comprehending all he said; and his voice, though gentle and sweet, was distinctly heard at a very extraordinary distance from the speaker.

In that charming volume, "The Little

Flowers of St. Francis," it is quaintly recorded: "That marvellous vessel of the Holy Ghost, St. Anthony of Padua, one of the chosen disciples and companions of St. Francis, who was called of St. Francis his Vicar, once preached in the Consistory before the Pope and his Cardinals; in which Consistory there were men of divers nations—namely, Greeks, Latins, French, Germans, Slavs, and English, and men speaking other divers tongues. Fired by the Holy Ghost, so efficaciously, so devoutly, so subtly, so sweetly, so clearly, and so plainly, did Anthony set forth the word of God, that all they which were present at the Consistory, of whatsoever divers tongues they were, clearly understood all his words distinctly, even as he had spoken in the language of each man among them. And they all were struck dumb with amaze; and it seemed as that ancient miracle of the Apostles had been renewed, when as at the time of the Pentecost they spoke by virtue of the Holy Ghost in every tongue. And they said one to another, with admiration and awe. 'Is not he who preaches come out of Spain? And how do we hear in his discourse every man of us the speech of his own land?' Likewise the Pope, considering and marvelling at the profundity of his words, said: 'Verily, this man is the Ark of the Covenant and the vehicle of the Holy Ghost.'"

Anthony appeared in a most opportune moment. The Church was sorely in need of him. St. Dominic had gone to his reward; the labors of St. Francis were at an end: he could only guide and encourage by his advice and his approval; and, at intervals, instil new life into his children and confer a benediction upon them by appearing, if but for a moment, in their midst. The honor and the glory that had been shared by St. Francis and St. Dominic were his now; for to Anthony fell the lot of continuing the work of these two illustrious patriarchs.

XII.—ANTHONY THE HAMMER OF HERETICS.

When Anthony girded on his armor and went forth to fight the good fight, the affairs of Europe, especially the religious affairs, were in a sad state. Heresy was rife. These heretics, known as Partorini, Cathari, Waldenses, Albigenses, and others almost too numerous to mention, were more or less united in an attempted revival of Manicheism; for the most part they taught the eternal existence of the principal of evil, denied the responsibility of the rational creature, recognized fatalism, and advocated the right of rebellion.

The secret societies, wherein the Jew was a rank element, had for their maxim: *Jura, perjura, secretum pandere noli.* — "Swear and forswear thyself, provided thou keep the secret." Their cry was: "Down with the Pope! Death to the Catholic Church!"

That was a sorry time. In his "History of France," Michelet says: "This Judea of France, as Languedoc has been called, was not only remarkable, like ancient Judea, for its bituminous pits and olive groves: it also had its Sodoms and Gomorrahs."

"Italy," says the old Franciscan chronicle, "was all overturned and filled with confusion by all the other nations, who came in to blooden their barbarous swords in her body; invited so to do by the Italians themselves, who called them in to take part in their intestine feuds, and who were all to be in the event their prey—as it turned out. And thus very soon there not only failed among them those sweet manners which used to make the Italians like to angels on earth, and placed them above all nations in courtesy and charity; but there died away also in them that blessed faith, for the love of which they had renounced the empire of the world, placing their necks under the most sweet yoke of Christ and of His Holy Roman Catholic Church. And as it happens so often that people take their customs from the company they keep, even the Italians drank of that horrible chalice of heresy and abomination; and, owing to license of life, which was then at its highest point, heretics began to multiply in that land."

Anthony seemed to have been singled out by Divine Providence to combat the prevailing evils of his time; to have had all his own sweet dreams, high hopes, and noble aspirations thwarted; to have been kept in the background, a silent, unknown man, until the moment when he was called to the front, to battle and to victory; for he achieved what perhaps he alone of all men could have achieved—a glorious and triumphant victory. How well he knew the nature and the requirements of his sacred office! He said:

"It behooves a preacher to lead on earth a heavenly life, in keeping with the truths he is charged to announce to the people. His conversation should only be concerning holy things; and his endeavors must tend to but one end—the salvation of souls. It is his duty to raise up the fallen, to console them that weep, to distribute the treasures of divine grace as the clouds send down their refreshing showers. And all this must he do with perfect humility and absolute disinterestedness. Prayer must be his chief delight; and the remembrance of the bitter Passion of Christ must ever accompany him, whether in joy or adversity. If he acts in this wise, the word of God, the word of peace and life, of grace and truth, will descend upon and flood him with its dazzling light."

He not only preached, he practised what he preached. The serenity and beauty of his countenance, the gentleness and meekness of his demeanor, were an example— a living and a lasting sermon unto all. Having once asked one of the brethren to go with him while he preached, the two went forth, and by and by returned,—Anthony not having uttered a word during all the time. The Brother, turning to him, said: "Why have you not preached?" And Anthony answered: "We *have* preached: our modest looks and the gravity of our behavior are as a sermon unto those who have followed us with their eyes."

He was absolutely without fear, and proved it on many occasions. Ezzelino of Treviso, having placed himself at the head of a party of Ghibellines, made himself master of Verona, Padua, and indeed most of the cities in Lombardy. For forty years this tyrant ruled there, and his bloody and horrible reign terrorized the people. He defied the anathemas of Popes Gregory IX., Innocent IV., and Alexander IV. Hearing that the long-suffering Paduans had revolted, he put to death in one day twelve thousand of the citizens.

Ezzelino lived at Verona. The horror of his presenee had caused the Veronese to fly, and the city was nearly depopulated. Armed guards, as savage as their master, patrolled the almost deserted streets. Anthony, going alone to Verona, sought audience of this monster. He entered the palace of Ezzelino and was conducted to the audience-chamber, where sat the bloodthirsty one upon a throne surrounded by his murderous troops. At a word from Ezzelino these human tigers would have fallen upon the defenceless Anthony and rent him limb from limb.

Anthony, undismayed, at once addressed the tyrant; assuring him that his plunderings, his sacrileges, were as a myriad tongues crying to Heaven for vengeance; and that his innumerable victims were living witnesses before God against him. The ferocious guards stood ready to spring upon the accuser; they awaited only the word. What was their astonishment when they saw merciless Ezzelino, pale and trembling, descending from his throne, and, putting a girdle about his neck for a halter, prostrating himself at the feet of Anthony, tearfully imploring him to intercede with God for the pardon of his sins!

When Anthony had departed, turning to his soldiers, Ezzelino said: "Be not astonished at my sudden change. I will tell you the truth. While Anthony was reproaching me I saw in his countenance a divine splendor; and I was so terrified that, if I had dared to take vengeance, I believe that I would have been suddenly carried off by demons and cast into hell."

Some time afterwards Ezzelino, wishing to test Anthony and see if he were really more than human, sent him a costly gift.

The gift-bearers were cautioned to press the treasure upon Anthony; but if he accepted it, they were to slay him at once; if he declined it, they were to come away and use no violence. These orders were obeyed. Bowing before the friar, they said: "Your faithful son Ezzelino has sent us to you. He earnestly recommends himself to your prayers, and beseeches you to accept this gift we offer you."

Anthony of course declined it, and begged that they would return to their master and say to him that it was God's wish that he should restore unto the impoverished whom he had laid waste, all that he had cruelly wrested from them; and that he should make this reparation before it was too late. With shame, they withdrew from the presence of the friar; and when they had reported to Ezzelino all that had passed between them, he replied, thoughtfully: "It is well. This is truly a man of

God. Leave him in peace. I care not what he says of me."

For a considerable period after this Ezzelino showed a disposition to mend his ways: he was less cruel, less bloodthirsty, a little more considerate of the rights and the feelings of his subjects. But after the death of Anthony he relapsed into his former mood, was in 1259 taken prisoner by the Confederate princes of Lombardy, and perished miserably in close confinement.

Anthony's success as a preacher was phenomenal and unparalleled. That fine old chronicler, John Peckham, says of it:

"From all parts of the city and its neighboring villages people flocked in crowds to hear the sermons of the great Franciscan. The law courts were closed, business was suspended, labor interrupted. All life and movement were concentrated at one point—the sermons and instructions of the mighty wonder-worker. Soon the churches could not contain the audiences: he had to preach in the open air. The plant, dried up by the heat of the sun, thirsts for the dew of the early morn; more lively and impatient was the desire of the Paduans for the coming dawn and the hour for which the conferences were announced. From midnight the city was in motion. Knights and great ladies, preceded by lighted torches, pressed round the temporary pulpit. A motley multitude covered the plain; while the bishop, accompanied by his clergy, presided at the services. The numbers often reached thirty thousand.

"At the hour fixed Anthony would appear, in outward demeanor modest and recollective, his heart burning with love. All eyes were fixed upon him; and when he began to speak, the crowds, hushed into silence, listened to his words with an immovable attention. At the conclusion of the discourse the enthusiasm of his hearers could not be contained: it burst forth in sobs, shouts of joy or applause, according to its effect upon each listener. The crowd would rush upon the Saint. Each one wished to see him closer, to kiss the hem of his habit, or his crucifix; some even went so far as to cut bits of cloth from his habit, to keep as relics. A body-guard of young men kept near him, to prevent his being crushed by his admirers.

"But the most admirable effects he achieved were the following: Enmities were appeased, and contending families publicly reconciled; usurers and thieves made restitution of their ill-gotten goods; great sinners struck their breasts in humble repentance; abandoned women fled from the haunts of vice and gave themselves up to penance. The confessionals were besieged; vice dissappeared, virtue revived; and within the space of a month the aspect of the ancient city [of Padua] was transformed."

Having entered the campaign, which proved a veritable holy war, within three months he became known to all as Anthony the Hammer of Heretics.

XIII.—ANTHONY'S SERMON ON THE MONASTIC LIFE.

The secret of Anthony's marvellous success we do not know; one may have thought it his voice, another his manner, and yet another his beautiful countenance. His piety, his fervor, his persuasive eloquence were all important aids; yet, perhaps, these alone might not have swayed the masses as he swayed them. He was master of the situation: alone, unrivalled— in a word, he was altogether irresistible.

It is a marvel that we know so little of one so great. One of the most conspicuous figures of his time, he is yet but as a shadow in the history of that time— or, rather, as a bright and shining light; illusive, like a Will-o'-the-wisp; startling and evasive, like the meteor. The truth is, he was not of this world.

The details of his life are scanty. Some one in the fourteenth century cried out, almost in despair: "We know not half of the beautiful actions of our hero! Most of them have been allowed to fall into oblivion, either by reason of the deplorable carelessness of his first biographers or through lack of authentic documents." This is the more surprising when we find the little testimony that is preserved to us aglow with almost boundless enthusiasm. In the Lucerne manuscript, "St. Antoine," Père Hilaire observes:

"His soul was like a fair garden fertilized by the showers of divine grace, where bloomed the sweetest flowers of Heaven, spreading around their fragrant odor. These flowers were meekness and humility, poverty and penance, fervor and zeal, wisdom and prudence. Beyond all praise were his eloquence, the gracefulness of his manners, his nobility of character, his gentleness and kindness. Whether in the pulpit or the confessional, with the clergy or laity, he everywhere and at all times evinced that spirit of prudence which gives the golden mean to all the virtues, and exhibited that utter forgetfulness of self which won him the love of all. In a word, he was indeed the beloved of God and men."

When Anthony went to Limoges, in 1226, he preached in the cemetery of St. Paul's Church, probably on All Souls' Day. A Benedictine writer has preserved the beautiful text, which was taken from the sixth verse of Psalm xxix: "In the evening weeping shall have place, and in the morning gladness." A brief exposition of the text has been found among his notes—most likely a synopsis of this sermon. "There is a threefold evening and a threefold morning," he says; "a threefold weeping and a threefold gladness. The threefold evening is, first, the sad evening of the fall of our first parents in Paradise; second, the sad evening of the passion and death of our Redeemer; and third, the sad evening of our own fast-approaching death. The threefold morning is, first, the glad morning of the birth of the Messias; second, the glad morning of the Lord's Resurrection; and third, the glad morning of our own future resurrection." Conceive what an effect this sermon must have produced as it fell from those inspired lips upon the ears of the mourners among the graves!

On the day following his address in the cemetery, Anthony preached in a Franciscan abbey, not far from the Church of St. Paul; and his notes of this sermon on the monastic life, happily preserved to us, are so full we gain from them a pretty clear idea of his treatment of a theme. On the text, "Who will give me wings like a dove, and I will fly and be at rest?" he says:

"Such is the cry of a soul that is weary

of this world and longs for the solitude and peace of the cloister life. It was of the religious life that Jeremias spoke when he said: 'Leave the cities, and dwell in the rock, you that dwell in Moab; and be ye like the dove that maketh her nest in the mouth of the hole in the highest place.' 'Leave the cities'—the sins and vices which dishonor, the tumult which prevents the soul from rising to God, and often even from thinking of Him. 'Leave the cities'; for it is written: 'I have seen iniquity and contradiction in the city. Day and night shall iniquity surround it upon its walls; and in the midst thereof are labor and injustice. And usury and deceits have not departed from its streets.' There is to be found iniquity against God and man; contradiction against the preacher of truth; labor in the ambitious cares of the world, injustice in its dealings, knavery and usury in its business transactions. 'Ye that dwell in Moab,'—that is, in the world, which is seated in pride as the city of Moab. All is pride in the world,—pride of the intellect, which refuses to humble itself before God; pride of the will, which refuses to submit to the will of God; pride of the senses, which rebel against reason and dominate it. . . .

"But to leave the world, to live remote from the tumult of cities, to keep one's self unspotted from their vices, is not sufficient for the religious soul. Hence the prophet adds: 'Dwell in the rock.' Now, this rock is Jesus Christ. Establish yourself in Him; let Him be the constant theme of your thoughts, the object of your affections. Jacob reposed upon a stone in the wilderness; and while he slept he saw the heavens opened, and conversed with angels, receiving a blessing from the Lord. Thus will it be with those who place their entire trust in Jesus Christ. They will be favored with heavenly visions; they will live in the company of angels; they will be blessed as Jacob was, 'to the north and south, to the east and west.' To the north, which is the divine breath mortifying the flesh and its concupiscences; to the east, which is the light of faith and the merit of good works; to the south, which is the full meridian splendor of wisdom and charity; to the west, which is the burial of the old man with his vices. But as to the soul which does not repose upon this rock, it can not expect to be blessed by the Lord.

"'And be ye like the dove that maketh her nest in the mouth of the hole in the highest place.' If Jesus Christ is the rock, the hole of the rock, in which the religious soul is to seek shelter and take up her abode, is the wound in the side of Jesus Christ. This is the safe harbor of refuge to which the Divine Spouse calls the religious soul when He speaks to her in the words of the Canticle: 'Arise, my love, my beautiful one, and come! . . . My dove in the clifts of the rock, in the hollow places of the wall.' The Divine Spouse speaks of the numberless clifts of the rock, but He also speaks of the deep hollow. There were indeed in His Body numberless wounds and one deep wound in His side; this leads to His Heart, and it is hither He calls the soul He has espoused. To her He extends His arms; to her He opens wide His sacred side and Divine Heart, that she may come and hide therein.

"By retiring into the clifts of the rock, the dove is safe from the pursuit of the birds of prey; and at the same time she prepares for herself a quiet refuge, where she may calmly repose and coo in peace. So the religious soul finds in the Heart of Jesus a secure refuge against the wiles and attacks of Satan, and a delightful retreat. But we must not rest merely at the entrance to the hole in the rock: we must penetrate its depths. At the mouth of the deep hollow—at the mouth of the wound in His side—we shall indeed find the Precious Blood which has redeemed us. This Blood pleads for us and demands mercy for us. But the religious soul must not stay at the entrance. When she has heard and understood the voice of the Divine Blood, she must hasten to the very source from which it springs—into the very innermost sanctuary of the Heart of Jesus. There she will find light, peace, and ineffable consolations.

"'And be ye like the dove that maketh her nest in the deep hollow of the rock.' The dove builds her nest with little pieces of straw she gathers up here and there. How are we to build up an abode in the Heart of Jesus? This Divine Saviour, who so mercifully gives us the place wherein we are to make our abode, furnishes us at the same time with the materials wherewith to construct it. O religious soul, dove beloved of Christ, behold those little pieces of straw which the world tramples under its feet! They are the virtues practised by thy Saviour and thy Spouse, of which He Himself has set thee an example—humility, meekness, poverty, penance, patience, and mortification. The world despises them as useless pieces of straw; nevertheless, they will be for thee the material wherewith to construct thy dwelling-place forever in the profound hollow of the rock—in the Heart of Jesus."

Thus Anthony preached to thousands and tens of thousands. And they followed him when he had finished speaking; for it seemed that they could never have enough of him. It was his custom to preface his sermons with this prayer, which he himself composed:

"O Light of the world, Infinite God, Father of eternity, Giver of wisdom and knowledge, and ineffable Dispenser of every spiritual grace; who knowest all things before they are made, who makest the darkness and the light: put forth Thy hand and touch my mouth, and make it as a sharp sword to utter eloquently Thy words. Make my tongue, O Lord! as a chosen arrow, to declare faithfully Thy wonders. Put Thy spirit, O Lord! in my heart, that I may perceive; in my soul, that I may retain; and in my conscience, that I may meditate. Do Thou lovingly, holily, mercifully, clemently and gently inspire me with Thy grace. Do Thou teach, guide and strengthen the comings in and goings out of my senses and my thoughts. And let Thy discipline instruct me even to the end, and the counsel of the Most High help me, through Thine infinite wisdom and mercy. Amen.''

So shone this light, with a glow as of fire from heaven, in the so-called Dark Ages.

XIV. — ANTHONY THE WONDER-WORKER.

That miracles have occurred, and are occurring even in our own day, there is no shadow of doubt. What is a miracle? According to Worcester, a miracle is "an effect of which the antecedent can not be referred to any secondary cause; an event or occurrence which can not be explained by any known law of nature; a deviation from the established law of nature; something not only superhuman, but preternatural; a prodigy, a wonder, a marvel"

Thousands of eye-witnesses bore testimony in their day to the wonders worked by Anthony in France and Italy. It would seem that his fame must have preceded him, and that wherever he went his approach must have been heralded and his appearance hailed with enthusiasm by expectant and animated throngs. This was not the case. Obedient to the voice of his superiors, he went wheresoever he was bidden; went alone and unannounced; a stranger in a strange land, unrecognized of any until he had lifted that voice whose persuasive eloquence no one was long able to withstand Then came his triumph, complete and overwhelming. Triumph followed upon triumph, until at last the land rang with his praises. On every hand he gave abundant proof of the divine power which he was called upon to exercise. Following in the footsteps of his Blessed Master, he healed the sick, raised the dead, and wakened the living to life everlasting.

Preaching once upon a time in the pulpit of the Church of St. Eusebius in Vicelli—a small Italian city, then an independent republic, like many another city of that day,—vast crowds pressed about him. Suddenly a great commotion arose. With difficulty a grief-stricken family bore toward him the body of one of their number, cut down in the prime of life. A great wail went up from the people. Anthony paused in his discourse, profoundly moved. Recollecting himself, he extended his hand towards the body and cried: "In the name of Christ I say unto you, young man, arise!" And immediately the youth arose from the dead, full of joy, restored to health and to the arms of those who had bewailed him.

Great is the number and the variety of the wonders worked by Anthony. Here are a few of them taken at random from the pages of his several chroniclers.

He was preaching in the cathedral at Montpellier, in the presence of the clergy and a vast multitude. It was Easter Sunday. In the midst of his discourse he suddenly remembered that he had been appointed to sing at Solemn High Mass in the choir of a neighboring convent chapel. He had forgotten this; he had even forgotten to find a substitute, and the hour of the Mass was at hand. This seemed to him an act of disobedience; and, in his distress, he drew his cowl over his face, sank back in the pulpit and remained silent for a long time. The people, in amazement, watched and waited. At the moment when he ceased speaking in the cathedral, though all the while visible to the congregation, he appeared in the convent choir among his brethren and sang his office. At the close of the service he recovered himself in the pulpit of the cathedral, and, as his chronicler says, finished his sermon "with incomparable eloquence."

Anthony had completed his "Commentary on the Psalms," the fruit of long vigilance and profound meditation. A novice, weary of the religious life and its ceaseless austerities, resolved to return to the world; and, coveting Anthony's precious manuscript, he captured it and fled. The young rascal could have had no sense of humor, or he would hardly have turned his back upon the cloister and sought the mixed society of the world, the flesh and the devil with a stolen copy of a "Commentary on the Psalms" as his companion. Probably he hoped to profit by it in a worldly way; but in this he was strangely thwarted. Upon discovering his loss, Anthony had, as ever, recourse to prayer. At that very moment the fleeing youth was confronted by a monstrous creature, that ordered him to return at once to the abbey and restore the "Commentary" to its author. This he was now only too glad to do. And the Saint, rejoiced at the recovery of his manuscript, as well as of the soul that was in peril, received the novice with every mark of affection. Nor was his loving-kindness ill bestowed; for the lad became one of the most favored of the faithful.

As St. Francis hushed the carolling birds in the Venetian lagoon, saying, "Cease your singing a little while, until we have rendered to God our homage of praise," so Anthony rebuked the clamoring frogs in a noisy pool at the Convent of Montpellier, and they thereafter observed a respectable silence at the hours of prayer.

At Puy-en-Velay he converted a notary of dissolute habits and violent temper. When they met in the streets Anthony would bow to the notary, and the latter would fly into a rage, believing that he was in mockery. Still Anthony saluted him reverently and more reverently; whereupon the notary cried, in a fury: "What does this mean? But for fear of the anger of God I would run you through with my sword." Then Anthony replied, with perfect composure: "O my brother! you do not know the honor in store for you. I envy your happiness. I longed for the martyr's palm: the Lord denied it to me, but He has revealed to me that this grace is reserved for you. When that blessed hour arrives, be mindful, I beseech you, of him who foretold it you." And it came to pass even as it had been predicted.

To a lady of rank who recommended herself to his prayers, Anthony said: "Be of good heart, my daughter, and rejoice; for the Lord will give you a son who, as a Friar Minor and a martyr, will shed lustre upon the Church." This prediction was likewise fnlfilled.

Many he delivered from sore temptations, and they were never again persecuted. To a poor sinner, overwhelmed with sorrow, who could find no voice with which to confess himself. Anthony said: "Go write down your sins, and bring me the parchment." The penitent did as he was bidden, returning with a tear-stained scroll. As he read out his sins one after the other, each disappeared from the parchment; and having reached the last of these, lo! the scroll was spotless.

At St. Junien, Anthony, who was about to address the public, predicted that the platform which had been erected for his use would collapse, but that no one would be injured. The fact was speedily verified.

One day, preaching to a great multitude in a large square in the city of Limoges, France, a violent storm gathered and filled the people with terror. They began to disperse in haste, when Anthony said: "Fear not: the storm will pass you by." So they remained; and, though the city was deluged, not a drop of rain fell in the square where Anthony was preaching.

At Brivé the Saint established a little hermitage similar to the one at Monte Paolo. Postulants joined him, seeking solitude and poverty. On one occasion, when they were in distress, a much-needed alms was sent them by a lady to whom they had reluctantly applied for aid. The lady's servant carried the gift to them through a severe storm; yet going and coming the servant walked dry-shod, and not one drop of water from the pouring clouds fell upon her.

One evening his companions at the hospice saw a band of marauders despoiling the field of one of the benefactors of the little community, and they hastened to complain to Anthony. "Fear not," said he. "'Tis but an artifice of the Evil One to distract you." On the morrow they found that the field had been untouched.

The Cathari of Rimini invited the Saint to a feast of poisons. His astounding success in bringing wanderers back to the fold filled them with hatred of him. He knew at once that a snare had been laid for him by the Cathari, and denounced them openly; thereupon they said to him: "Either you believe the words of the Gospel or you do not. If you believe them, why hesitate to eat? Is it not written, 'In My name they shall cast out devils; they shall handle serpents; and if they shall drink any deadly thing, it shall not hurt them'? If you do not believe the Gospel to be true, why do you preach it? Take, therefore, and eat. If you go unhurt, we swear to embrace the Catholic faith." Blessing the viands, the servant of God ate and was unharmed; and all those who beheld the miracle returned into the fold.

Paralysis and epilepsy he cured with the Sign of the Cross.

At Gemona, near Udine, where he was erecting a small convent on the model of the Portiuncula, he one day hailed a peasant who was passing with an ox team, and begged that a load of bricks might be brought him. The peasant, not knowing who addressed him, and not caring to be pressed into Anthony's service, said: "I can not help you, for I am carrying a corpse." The truth is, the peasant's son lay sleeping in the bottom of the cart. When the peasant, a little later, attempted to waken the boy so as to tell him how he had fooled the friar, he found that his son was dead. Then he ran to Anthony and implored him to restore the life of the boy; and Anthony making the Sign of the Cross over the body, the youth arose and blessed him.

Often, under the influence of his exhortations, penitents were moved to tears and convulsive sobs. To such he would say—to quote from his notes: "Poor sinner, why despair of thy salvation, since all here speaks of mercy and of love? Behold the two advocates who plead thy cause before the tribunal of Divine Justice: a Mother and a Redeemer,—Mary, who presents to her Son her heart transfixed with the sword of sorrow; Jesus, who presents to His Father the wounds in His feet and hands, and His Heart pierced by the soldier's lance. Take courage; with such a mediator, with such an intercessor, Divine Mercy can not reject thee."

Who could resist this appeal, or fail to find strength and consolation in it?

XV.—ANTHONY PREACHES TO THE FISHES.

Again I return to that garden of delights, "The Little Flowers of St. Francis." So delicate, so dainty, so fragrant are these flowers one can not pass them by unnoticed. The lips of the devout fashioned them, and for two centuries they blossomed wherever the lovers of the Saint were gathered together; then they were carefully culled and brought from near and far; and a bouquet was made of them, and it was called "The Little Flowers of St. Francis."

Therein we find that "our Blessed Lord and Saviour Jesus Christ, desiring to set forth the great sanctity of His most faithful servant, St. Anthony, how devout a thing it was to hear his preaching and his holy doctrines, He reproved the folly of heretics and infidels through unreasoning beasts—notably the fishes,—as of old in the Bible

He chid the ignorance of Balaam through the mouth of the ass. Hence St. Anthony being at Rimini, where there was a great multitude of heretics, desiring to bring them back to the light of the true faith and to the ways of virtue, for many days did preach and set forth to them the faith of Christ and of the Holy Scriptures. But they, not only consenting not to his holy words, but even, like hardened and obstinate sinners, refusing to hearken unto him, the Saint one day, by divine inspiration, went forth to the banks of the river close beside the sea; and, standing thus upon the shore betwixt sea and stream, he began to speak in the guise of a sermon in the name of God unto the fishes. 'Hear the word of God, ye fishes of the sea and of the stream, since heretics and infidels are loath to listen to it.'

"And, having uttered these words, suddenly there came towards him so great a multitude of fishes—great, small, and middle-sized—as had never been seen in that sea or in that stream, or of the people round about; and all held their heads up out of the water, and all turned attentively towards the face of Anthony. And the greatest peace and meekness and order prevailed; insomuch that next the shore stood the lesser fish, and after them the middle fish, and still after them, where the water was deepest, stood the larger fish.

"The fish being thus ranged in order, St. Anthony began solemnly to preach, speaking thus: 'My brothers the fish, you are greatly bounden, so far as in you lies, to thank your Creator that He hath given you so noble an element for your habitation; so that at your pleasure you have fresh waters and salt; and He hath given you many shelters against storm. He hath also given you a clear and lucid element, and food by which you may live. God, your courteous and benign Creator, when He created you, commanded you to grow and multiply; and He gave you His blessing. Then when the great flood swallowed up the world, and all the other animals were destroyed, God preserved you only without injury or harm. Almost hath He given you wings, that you may roam whithersoever it pleases you. To you was it granted, by God's command, to preserve the prophet Jonah, and after the third day to cast him up upon the land safe and sound. You offered tribute to our Lord Jesus Christ, which He, poor and lowly, had not wherewithal to pay. You were the food of the everlasting King Christ Jesus before the Resurrection, and again after it, by a strange mystery; for the which things greatly are you bounden to praise and bless God, which hath given you such great and so many benefits, more than to any other creatures.'

"Upon these and other familiar words and the teachings of St. Anthony, the fishes began to ope their mouths and to bow their heads; and by these and other signs of reverence, according as it was possible to them, they praised God. Then St. Anthony, seeing such reverence in the fishes towards God their Creator, rejoiced in spirit, cried aloud and said: "Blessed be the eternal God, since fishes of the water honor Him far more than heretic men, and the unreasoning beasts more readily hearken to His word than faithless men.' And as St. Anthony continued his preaching, the multitude of fishes was increased yet more, and none departed from the place which he had filled.

"Upon this miracle the people of the town began to hasten forth, and among them were also the aforesaid heretics; the which, seeing so manifest and marvellous a miracle, felt their hearts sorely pricked, and they fell with one accord at St. Anthony's feet to hear his word. Then St.

Anthony began to preach of the Catholic faith; and so nobly did he discourse that he converted all those heretics and turned them to the true faith of Christ; and all the faithful were comforted with great joy, and were confirmed in their faith. And this done, St. Anthony dismissed the fishes with the blessing of God; and they all departed with marvellous signs of rejoicing, and likewise the people. And then St. Anthony stayed in Rimini for many days, preaching and reaping a spiritual harvest of souls."

XVI.—ANTHONY AND THE ISRAELITE.

There dwelt at Bourges, the capital of Berry, in France, an Israelite who was of all Israelites the most bitter foe of the Catholic Church. He was the leader of the anti-Christian movement, an earnest worker in opposition to every doctrine that Anthony taught. Guillard the Jew was not an ignorant and blind bigot: he was a man of intelligence, an honest doubter. Often he had listened to the preaching of Anthony, yet he was not convinced. Shall we not say that it was his misfortune rather than his fault that he remained without the fold and persistently assumed an attitude of antagonism?

The dogma of the real presence of Our Lord in the Blessed Sacrament was naturally his chief stumbling-block. Much he could accept and much consider in a calm spirit of philosophical inquiry; but the Eucharist, transubstantiation—the perpetual miracle—was in his estimation past belief. For this miracle he demanded miraculous proof.

"The Turk does not question the word of Mohammed," observed Anthony to this fellow of Didimus the Doubter; "the philosopher accepts the philosophy of Aristotle; but you, who pride yourself upon being a worthy Israelite, will not accept the testimony of the Son of God."—"I must see for myself, with these very eyes, before I can believe," replied the doubting Thomas. There are many who, like him, must put their finger in the wounds before they are convinced of the living truth.

One day Guillard said to Anthony: "Brother Anthony, if by some tangible, outward sign you can confirm the truth you have demonstrated by reasoning, I will abjure my ancient creed and embrace yours. Do you consent?" In order to save a soul one may make great concessions; nor was it beneath the dignity of Anthony to offer visible proof to an anxious and inquiring eye. "I consent," said he.—"I have a mule," added the Jew: "I will keep him for three days under lock and key, and in all that time feed him nothing. At the end of the third day I will bring him to the largest public square in the city; and there, in the presence of all the assembled people, I will offer him a feed of oats. You, on the other hand, will come carrying the Host, which, as you believe, is the true body of the Son of God. If the mule refuses the proffered food in order to prostrate himself before the monstrance, I will become a Catholic, and no longer question the truth of the doctrine taught by the Catholic Church."

Here was a direct challenge, and it was not declined. Anthony felt that his victory was assured. The reward of that victory was an immortal soul. For three days the young apostle devoted himself to fasting and prayer. Not for one moment did he lose faith in the success of the miracle he was about to work, but he dared not attempt it without solemn preparation. Meanwhile Guillard and his companions were so sure of Anthony's total defeat and discomfiture that there was much merriment at the wonder-worker's expense; and the interest in the approaching test increased from hour to hour.

The eventful day arrived. Guillard and his friends trooped into the public square with smiles and laughter, so confident were they that the famishing mule would instantly abandon himself to his oats. The immense throngs who had gathered to witness the impending spectacle were consumed with curiosity. As Anthony slowly approached, bearing reverently the Sacred Host, his eyes cast down, his air devotional, a great hush fell upon the multitude. He was followed by a large crowd of the faithful, singing canticles and whispering prayers.

The mule was then led forward, and the oats laid temptingly before him. At that moment Anthony drew near, bearing the monstrance. Turning towards the dumb brute, he exclaimed: "In the name of thy Creator, whose body I, though unworthy, hold in my hands, I enjoin and command thee, O being deprived of reason! to come hither instantly and prostrate thyself before thy God; so that by this sign unbelievers may know that all creation is subject to the Lamb who is daily immolated upon our altars." In the same moment Guillard and his friends presented the oats to the famished beast. Without taking the smallest notice of the food, the mule, turning away, walked to the feet of Anthony, and, bending his knees, knelt before the Blessed Sacrament and remained there in an attitude of adoration.

Great was the enthusiasm among the faithful. The heretics fled away in fright and hid themselves for shame; they dared not face the one who had proved that prayer is more powerful than the laws of nature. Many were so moved by the wondrous spectacle that, though they had long wandered from the path of duty, they returned into the fold. Guillard likewise sought admission, for he could no longer doubt; and with him came his household. He publicly attested his faith, and in gratitude erected a church upon the spot where the miracle had taken place; and that monument endures to this hour. As late as 1850 a block of marble, carved to represent a mule in the attitude of devotion, was discovered in the wall of the façade of the church built by Guillard, and consecrated in 1231 by Archbishop Simon de Sully.

Pierre Rosset, a Doctor of the University of Paris and a poet of the fifteenth century; Wadding, in his "Annals of the Friars Minor"; and Benedict Mazzara, in his "Franciscan Legends," bear witness to the authenticity of this memorial of a miracle. Toulouse and Rimini claim a like honor with Bourges, and there are those who have believed that the miracle was repeated. The evidence is cloudy and conflicting in these cases, but there is no shadow of doubt that Anthony the wonder-worker worked that wonder in the ancient city of Bourges; and that Guillard the Israelite then and there built the Church of St. Peter in honor of his glorious conversion.

XVII.—ANTHONY AND THE CHRIST-CHILD.

Let us not be disconcerted if we find several cities contending for the honor to which one only is entitled. Since Homer's death it has been the fate of the distinguished poet to be claimed by many and various peoples as father, brother, son; though while living in obscurity the devoted soul was suffered to endure neglect. It is not surprising that the miracles of Anthony have not always been definitely located. Some of them may have been repeated in two or more localities. Tradition is more or less elastic; it sometimes grows with what it feeds on. What is of utmost importance is the proof of a miracle; it matters less where it actually took place.

In Anthony we see embodied the beauty of holiness. There is one who has borne witness to the truth of this, for he was an eye-witness. The blessed privilege he enjoyed should have immortalized him, and yet the authorities are not united as to his identity.

Anthony founded the monastery of Arcella Vecchia, without the walls, about a mile distant from Padua. There he loved to dwell; but as his duties called him into the city daily, and when preaching or hearing confessions in the evening he was often detained until the city gates were closed, he found it necessary to seek a lodging which he could occupy at his leisure. This he found, as Azevedo informs us, at the house of Tiso, or Tisone, one of the ancient family of counts of Camposampiero, famous in the records of their time.

That a miracle was performed somewhere no chronicler doubts; but Azevedo seems to have had insufficient proof of the grounds for his statement that it took place in Padua.

Wadding, on the other hand, does not attempt to locate it; but Father Bonaventure de St. Amable, a Carmelite of the seventeenth century, on the authority of ancient documents existing in his time, names without hesitation Châteauneuf — the modern Châteauneuf-la-Foret—as the hallowed spot. The legend is perhaps the best known in the life of the Saint, as it is certainly the most beautiful; and it has been a favorite subject for the art of the best masters during the last eight hundred years.

Accepting the hospitality of the Lord of Châteauneuf, who, according to the "Annals de Limousin," dearly loved St. Anthony and his holy Order, he retired to his chamber and began the prayerful vigil that usually extended far into the night. His host, who was in an adjoining apartment, was startled by a light as of a conflagration that poured from under the door of Anthony's room. Hastening to the door, but fearing to enter lest he should disturb his guest, he listened for a few moments. Hearing voices, he became agitated; and, riveting his eye at a crevice, he beheld a vision that filled him with awe and wonder.

Anthony knelt at a table where a large volume lay open; upon the volume, or above it, stood a child of such surpassing loveliness that the gazer's heart leaped within him, and his lips would have cried out for joy but that some mysterious influence enjoined silence upon him. The body of the infant was effulgent: a soft glow was diffused on every side. The lustre of that countenance was ineffable. The radiant being seemingly reposed upon the air; and, from a soft veil of vapor that emitted a celestial fragrance, he leaned fondly upon the bosom of the friar, and with hands of exquisite loveliness delicately caressed him. Soft music, mingled with voices of heavenly tenderness and the flutter of invisible wings, betokened the presence of angelic visitors.

The child, who was the Christ-Child, whispered in the ear of Anthony; and, as the Saint turned to the door, the master of Châteauneuf knew that his presence was detected. So when Anthony met him on the morrow these words passed between them; the Limousin chronicler records them in their brevity and simplicity: "Father, what did Our Lord say to you?"—"He revealed to me that your house will flourish and enjoy great prosperity so long as it remains faithful to mother Church; but that it will be overwhelmed with misfortune and become extinct when it goes over to heresy."

In the seventeenth century the then Lord of Châteauneuf espoused the cause of the Calvinists, and in the fall of that house the prophecy was fulfilled. As for Anthony, one ever associates him with the Christ-Child who nestles in his arms. From the holy visitations of the Divine Infant he gathered inspiration, and it was he who said: "The Sacred heart is a fountain of supernatural life; a golden altar whereon is burning, night and day forever, incense that ascends in clouds of fragrance toward the skies, and envelops and embalms the earth"

XVIII. S. A. G.

Some folk think the letters are mystical. Though their significance is known to many, there are very many more to whom they convey no meaning. You will usually find them, if they are visible, on the addressed side of an envelope, down in the lower left-hand corner. I say when they are visible; for some who use them seem afraid to use them openly, and so the letters are written in the upper right-hand corner of the envelope, where the postage-stamp covers them; or they are inscribed on the underside of the lapel of the envelope, and hidden away.

It is a pretty cult, a sweet devotion, a symbol of faith and trust; and its votaries, who were shy enough at first—and perhaps with reason, for bigotry was rampant but a few years ago,—now grow bolder; and their numbers multiply daily, hourly, and are scattered even unto the four quarters of the globe.

S. A. G.! What do these letters stand for? The question has been asked me a thousand times. Perhaps the letters, down in their cozy corner, were passed unnoticed for a time; then it was discovered that they were not the initials of the writer; interest was now excited, and at last curiosity refused to be satisfied until the mystery was solved.

S. A. G.! St. Anthony guide; or, St. Anthony guard. But why St. Anthony guide? It is the peculiar privilege of the Saint to guard and guide all travellers, and especially all toilers of the sea and all who are exposed to the peril of wind and wave. He is the rescuer and restorer of the "lost, strayed, or stolen." Not a day passes, not an hour, but voices of the distressed are crying to him for help in a search after something that is mislaid. And they do not cry in vain. There is testimony enough in proof of this to fill a library.

Is it a foolish office to heed these sometimes trivial requests? Every answer is an answer to prayer, and the answer to prayer is the bulwark of our faith. Thus the wonder-worker works a perpetual wonder; it is an incessant miracle, that brings joy to myriads of grateful hearts.

Every year the number of letters placed under the guidance of dear St. Anthony increases. The writers of letters who use the initials S. A. G. seem to have formed an involuntary brotherhood; they are unconscious members of another order of St. Francis, who thus proclaim, even unto the ends of the earth, their absolute faith in St. Anthony and his readiness to aid them. That he has a special interest in the transportation of written messages is twice proved in his own case. The facts read like fairy tales—but, then, let us remember his life was one long fairy tale filled full of wonders.

Anthony, on one occasion being greatly in need of rest, wished to retire for a little season to a soltitude about ten miles from Padua, known as Campo San Pietro. With this end in view, he wrote to his minister provincial begging that he might be permitted to repair thither. The letter written, he went to the superior of the monastery and asked that some trusty messenger be charged with the delivery of his letter, and his request was at once granted. Returning to his cell to procure the letter and deliver it to the messenger, he found it had disappeared. He searched for it in vain. Unable to find it, he took it as a sign that his duty lay where he was, and he dismissed all thoughts of visiting Campo San Pietro. Shortly afterward, turning again to his desk where he had left the letter, he found the answer lying there,—the answer written by his minister provincial, and freely granting his request. Was it a celestial messenger that favored him? It is now Anthony's turn to favor one of his devoted clients.

In 1729 Antonio Dante, a Spanish merchant, left Spain for South America and established his business in Lima, Peru. His wife, who remained in Spain, wrote to him repeatedly without receiving a reply. In great anxiety she went one day to the Church of St. Francis, at Oviedo; here was a large statue of St. Anthony. She had with her a letter addressed to her absent husband. In all simplicity and with perfect confidence, she placed that letter in the hands of the statue and said: "St. Anthony, I pray thee let this letter reach him, and obtain for me a speedy reply."

The next day she returned to renew her prayer. Seeing a letter still in his hands, and believing it to be the one she had placed there, the poor soul began to weep;

and, crying aloud, she said: "St. Anthony, why have you kept the letter which I wrote to my husband, instead of sending it to him, as I asked you?" Her boisterous grief attracted the attention of the Brother sacristan, who came to ask the cause of it. When he had heard her story he said: "I have in vain tried to take that letter from the hand of St. Anthony. See if he will give it to you. She took the letter from the hand of the image without difficulty, and at the same moment there fell from the sleeve of the statue three hundred golden coins. The amazed sacristan hastened into the adjoining monastery, called the friars into the church, where the bewildered woman was still waiting; and in their presence, before the high altar, the letter was opened and read. It ran as follows:

LIMA, July 23, 1729.

MY DEAR WIFE:—For some time I have been expecting a letter from you, and been in great trouble at not hearing from you. At last your letter has come, and given me joy. It was a Father of the Order of St. Francis who brought it to me. You complain that I have left your letters unanswered. I assure you that when I received none I believed you to be dead. So you may imagine my happiness at the arrival of your last one. I answer by the same religious, and send you three hundred golden crowns, which will suffice for your support until my approaching return. In the hope of soon being with you, I pray God for you, commend myself to my dear patron St. Anthony, and ardently desire that you may continue to send me tidings of yourself.

  Your most affectionate,
      ANTONIO DANTE.

The original letter, written in Spanish, is preserved at Oviedo.

XIX.—ANTHONY IN PADUA.

Anthony had long been a wanderer. From Portugal he travelled into Spain, Morocco, Sicily. He journeyed from Messina to Assisi; from Assisi to Monte Paolo, Toulouse, Puy-en-Velay, Limoges, Rome, Rimini, Venice, Ferrara, Mantua, and elsewhere. But of all the cities he visited and of all the peoples he ministered unto, his name was destined to become associated with Padua and the Paduans.

The Padua of to-day is not the Padua of old: it is naturally more or less modernized; yet, happily, a delightful flavor of antiquity still abides there, and is perceptible in all its nooks and corners. When I first visited Padua I was a pilgrim and a stranger. One may be ever a pilgrim in that hallowed land, but never twice a stranger. Alighting at the station, I wandered through the streets, suffering myself to be piloted—by my Good Angel it may have been—till I came to the inn with the sign of the Three White Crosses, and I abode there. The fifty thousand people of Padua left me to myself, and I went my way as if I were invisible to any. This shrine seems to be the least commercial of them all, and yet it is one of the most famous and the most popular.

How soon one does Padua as a tourist: devouring it, as it were; *bolting* it as the hungry sight-seer *bolts* everything visible! Of course there is a memory and an indigestion after all is over, and the fagged tourist packs himself home and sits down to think. One does it in a day—so much of Padua as is in the guide-book. There is a memory of lovely churches and the tombs of saints, and old walls covered with very ancient frescoes and other works of art,— here Giotto was in his glory. And there is a memory of a host of college boys wandering to and fro with their arms upon one another's shoulders. A world-famous University, that has been flourishing half a thousand years, is located here.

Somehow, one can not help thinking of Enrico and his Italian "School-Boy's Journal"—that most charming of the works of De Amicis—when one falls in with these Paduan students, with their troubadour faces and airs and graces—albeit they are not half so interesting as little Enrico. Oh, the power, the beauty, the fervor and the pathos of that book—"Cuore," by Edmondo de Amicis! Read it, if you have not read it; there you will see the heart of Young Italy laid bare.

The great circular piazza of the city is wreathed with a double row of statues, commemorating in marble the famous—or perhaps in some cases the infamous—graduates of the memorable University.

In Anthony's day Padua was a very different town. Now it languishes in its comfortable age; then it was the abode of luxury, the haunt of vice. Debauchery and usury flourished; family feuds were rife, and God was forgotten. At Rimini, Bourges, Toulouse, Anthony had warred against heresy; at Padua it was the sensuous and sensual and dissolute life of the people he was called upon to reform. Fearlessly he struck at the root of the evil; face to face he attacked the depravity of those high in office; hand to hand he wrestled with every obstacle that was raised before him, and overthrew them each and all. He was gentle, but firm; and his manner was so majestic, his argument so convincing, and his denunciation so terrible, that no one could long withstand him.

He put an end to the most painful family contentions, and to the scandalous quarrels of political factions. Guelph and Ghibelline were reconciled; those who had been long estranged fell upon one another's necks and exchanged the kiss of peace. Those who seemed unapproachable were approached by him; those who were deaf to all others gave him an attentive ear.

Sixty-four years after his conversion by St. Anthony, a once notorious brigand gave to the Friars Minor the following remarkable narrative of his personal experience:

"I was a brigand by profession and one of a band of robbers. There were twelve of us living in the forest, whence we issued to waylay travellers and commit every kind of depredation. The reputation of Anthony, his preaching and his miraculous deeds, penetrated even to our ears in the depths of the forest. Rumor compared him to the Prophet Elias. It was said his words were so ardent and efficacious as to resemble the spark that falling into the sheaves of corn sets them aflame and consumes them.

"We resolved to disperse ourselves one day amongst the crowd in order to test the truth of these assertions. While he spoke another voice seemed to resound in our ears—the voice of remorse. After the sermon all the twelve of us, contrite and repentant, threw ourselves at his feet. He called down upon us the divine pardon, but not without warning us that if we unfortunately relapsed into our old ways we should perish miserably. This prediction was verified. A few did relapse, and ended their days on the gallows. Those who persevered fell asleep in the peace of the Lord.

"As for myself, St. Anthony imposed upon me the penance of making a pilgrimage twelve times to the tomb of the Apostles. To-day I have completed my twelfth visit; and I feel confident that, according to his promise and through his merits, I shall meet him above." The chronicle adds: "Tears and sobs interrupted the old man's last words."

Anthony is the glory of Padua, and gloriously has Padua enshrined him. In all her strange, eventful history there is no name that shines like his. He was one of the two who did more for the enlightenment, the humanizing and the harmonizing of the hordes of the Middle Ages than all the rest besides.

Frédéric Morin, in his "St. François et les Franciscains," says: "Modern Europe has no idea of all it owes to St. Francis of Assisi." Montalembert has proved by indisputable facts that "the victory of Christianity over neo-paganism in the Middle Ages was chiefly due to the gallant efforts of the two new religious bodies that sprang up in the thirteenth century."

In the introduction of his life of "St. Elizabeth of Hungary" Montalembert says: "The children of St. Dominic and St.

Francis spread themselves over Italy (then torn by so many disorders), striving to reconcile rival factions, to vindicate truth and confute error; acting as supreme arbitrators, yet judging all things in a spirit of charity. In 1233 they could be seen traversing the peninsula, armed with crosses, incense, and olive branches; upbraiding the cities and princes with their crimes and enmities; and the people, for a time at least, bowed before this sublime mediation." Cesare Cantu, in his "Histoire Universelle," adds: "At the head of the peacemakers we must place St. Francis of Assisi and his disciple, St. Anthony of Padua."

Anthony preached peace and he restored it. His constant cry was: "No more war; no more hatred and bloodshed, but peace! *God wills it!*" And there was peace. He was not quite alone in his noble efforts toward the reconciliation of all mankind: the parish clergy, the sons of St. Benedict and St. Dominic, as well as the sons of St. Francis, rallied at his call and mustered under his generalship. It was a holy war and a triumphant one. Among these soldiers of the Cross was one Luke Belludi, a preacher of eloquence and power, who received the habit from St. Francis himself, and who was one of Anthony's most devoted followers. His ashes lie buried by the side of those of the Saint he loved, in that wonderful shrine in Padua.

He had his willing workers there in Padua and elsewhere, but the burden fell upon the shoulders of Anthony. And what a burden of responsibility, of patient endurance, of calm judgment and wise and deliberate action it was! Yet all the while he was devoted to his mission: day and night he was in the pulpit or the confessional, or by the bedside of the sick and dying; and none of the thousand cares of the sacred ministry was neglected by him.

Ever forgetful of self, it is said that often and often he would toil until evening with no other nourishment, and no thought of other nourishment, than the Blessed Bread he had received from the altar at dawn. And all this was for the love of his people, for the honor of Padua and the greater glory of God.

XX.—THE PASSING OF ANTHONY.

Anthony having chosen Padua as his place of residence, because, as his biographer, John Peckham, says, "of the faith of its inhabitants, their attachment to him, and their devotion to the Friars Minor," he there ended his life-work in his thirty-sixth year of grace.

How he loved Padua! A fortnight before his death, having ascended a hill overshadowing the city, he gazed down upon it in all its beauty; and, stretching forth his hands above its marble palaces, its domes, and lofty bell-towers, embosomed in bowers of foliage; while the incense of its blossoming gardens was wafted to him, and the ripening corn-fields and the vineyards framed it all in a frame of gold and green and purple, he exclaimed in rapture: "Blessed be thou, O Padua, for the beauty of thy site! Blessed be thou for the harvest of thy fields! Blessed also shalt thou be for the honor with which Heaven is about to crown thee!" What honor? At that moment, in a vision, he beheld the celestial city, and through the gates of Padua the beloved his soul was to pass hence forever.

It was while on his way to the heights of Campo San Pietro, a few miles from Padua, passing through a wood, the property of his friend Don Tiso, Anthony discovered a walnut-tree of gigantic proportions; here was deep shadow, layer upon layer, among branches as large as the rafters of a hall. Nothing could be more inviting; for only the birds nested there, while the butterflies fluttered in the sunshine that environed it. It was a green island in a golden sea; a place of refuge and refreshment for the world-weary.

Having foreknowledge of his death, Anthony bethought him of this retreat.

With pliant boughs he wove a wall of verdure, and fashioned a little cell between earth and heaven,—the daintiest oratory that ever was, and a couch for one who was in the world but not of it. The old masters have pictured him as in a nest among the spreading branch, and have painted him with childlike simplicity as brooding there. Probably his leafy cell was a little heaven of detachment, where nothing ever broke in upon his meditations. His faithful allies, Brother Luke Belludi and Brother Roger, kept watch with him,—two silent sentinels standing between him and the outer world.

Once a day he descended from his airy solitude and broke bread with the two Brothers who attended him; it seemed to be more a matter of form than of necessity. He no longer was of the earth as we are, but was a spirit bearing about a fragile shell of clay that was soon to be laid aside, a useless and abandoned thing. His waking hours were passed in prayer and in the completion of his commentaries. He spoke not, nor was he ever known to smile: he was absorbed in preparation for his final flight.

One day, when he had descended to break his fast with his companions, he fainted at their rustic board. At first the Brothers thought him in ecstasy—for his ecstasies were frequent now; but, seeing the shadow of death upon him, they hastened to assist him to a couch of green shoots close at hand. Having recovered consciousness, and seeing the Brothers bending over him in tears, he begged that he might at once be taken to the monastery at Padua, there to die among his brethren, supported by their presence and their prayers. He was tenderly placed in a passing peasant's cart, and the sad procession started. But so great was his exhaustion when they reached Arcella—the Convent of Poor Clares, near the gates of the city,—that the Brothers besought him to alight there to seek the rest he stood so much in need of. With difficulty he was assisted into a small hospice adjoining the convent, where dwelt three or four Friars Minor who acted as chaplains to the daughters of St. Clare.

By this time Anthony was beginning to lose consciousness; but, recovering himself for a little while, he made his last confession. When the friars proposed to anoint him he said: "I already possess that unction within myself; but it is good to receive it outwardly."

While Extreme Unction was being administered he recited with the brethren prayers for the dying and the Penitential Psalms, and received the absolution. Then, filled with a heavenly joy that was like an ecstasy, to the wonder of those about him, he sang alone, and in a clear, full voice, his favorite hymn:

O gloriosa Domina
Excelsa super sidera,
Qui te creavit provide
Lactasti sacro ubere.

Quod Eva tristis abstulit,
Tu reddis almo germine:
Intrent ut astra flebiles,
Cœli fenestra facta es.

Tu Regis alti janua,
Et porta lucis fulgida:
Vitam datam per Virginem,
Gentes redemptæ, plaudite.

Gloria tibi, Domine,
Qui natus es de Virgine,
Cum Patre et Sancto Spiritu
In sempiterna sæcula.

Having ceased singing, he raised his eyes to heaven with a gaze that startled his companions; it was as if those eyes were filled with some wondrous vision. Brother Roger, in whose arms he was supported, said: "What do you see?" And Anthony answered, still gazing in rapture: "I behold my God!" For about half an hour he was lost in contemplation of the beatific vision;

and then, like a weary child, he fell into a deep sleep—and woke no more.

At the moment when his soul was set free from its earthly tabernacle Anthony appeared to Don Thomas, the Abbot of St. Andrew's at Vercelli, who was at the time sitting alone in the room. His former pupil entered and said to him: "See, Father Abbot, I have left my burden near the gates of Padua, and am hastening to mine own country." He then passed his hand caressingly across the throat of the Abbot, who was suffering from a severe chronic affliction; and the throat was permanently cured. Thereupon Anthony disappeared.

The Abbot, surprised at the sudden entrance and the exit of Anthony, hastened after him to beg him to remain a little while a guest; but, throwing open the door of his chamber, no Anthony was visible. Those who were waiting in the ante-chamber had seen nothing of him; nor had any one at St.

Andrew's, save only the Abbot, any knowledge of Anthony. Then the Abbot knew that the burden Anthony had left at Padua was his body; and that the home to which he was hastening was not Portugal, but Paradise.

Efforts were made to keep Anthony's death a secret. He was the popular idol of all Italy, and not alone of Italy: he had wielded greater personal influence than almost any man of his time. He was not only respected by the masses, but he was listened to with rapt attention by the representatives of all classes, from the peer to the peasant. He was loved by all, reverenced by all; he was fairly worshipped by the vast multitude of his faithful followers. And, therefore, it was deemed wise to keep his death a secret — for a time at least, — lest the populace should be distracted and demoralized by so terrible a blow.

Man proposes! Hardly had his bright

spirit taken its flight when the children of Padua—the children he so dearly loved,—as if inspired, rushed about the streets in a kind of frenzy, crying out: "Our Saint is dead! St. Anthony is dead!" Consternation followed; the whole city was plunged in desperate grief; and still worse was to follow.

The body of Anthony was a precious treasure coveted by all. As the dying gaze of St. Francis rested upon Assisi, the city of his soul, whose portals he was not again permitted to enter in the flesh, so Anthony, homesick and heart-sick for his Padua, gave up the ghost without her gates. Had Anthony entered the city and breathed his last in the monastery of his Order, there could have arisen no question as to the ultimate disposition of his remains. But he fell by the wayside, as it were; therefore the Poor Clares, in whose humble hospice he died, claimed the honor of enshrining his remains; so did his brethren, the Friars Minor of Padua; so also did the suburbs and the magistracy of Padua promptly forward their claims. Thus it happened that the body of the Saint who strove to bring peace into the world once more, became the source of violent contention.

John Peckham describes the grief of the Poor Clares at the death of Anthony. "Alas!" they cried, "unhappy we! O tender Father of our souls, taken forever from your daughters, why has death spared us for this cruel blow? Our poverty contented us and we counted ourselves rich when we could hear you preach to us the Gospel of the Lord."

Then one of the nuns sought to console the others in these words: "Why shed useless tears? It is not the dead we are bewailing, but an immortal, the companion of angels, an inhabitant of heaven. A great consolation will flow for us out of this painful separation if we can keep him here amongst us—a joy we could not have whilst he lived."

The Poor Clares sent a deputation to the magistrates and nobles of Padua, beseeching them to lend their influence to the end that the body of Anthony might be retained in their convent. The friars, immediately upon learning of his death, hastened to Arcella with the intention of removing the remains at once to their monastery of Santa Maria. "It was his wish," they said, in proof of their right to possess the body. And so it *was* his wish; yet the people of Capodiponte, where Arcella was situated, openly sided with the Poor Clares, and resolved that the Friars Minor should not carry away with them the blessed remains. The friars appealed to the bishop, who decided in their favor; but when the enthusiastic Paduans went forth to bring away the body, they were met by the armed partisans of the Poor Clares, and bloodshed seemed imminent and inevitable.

At length the bishop persuaded the combatants to declare a truce until the provincial—who was absent at the time, and had been sent for—should return. Still this did not suffice. That very night, while the friars at the hospice of the Poor Clares were watching beside the dead behind barricaded doors, the excited populace, eager to get a view of the body, if not to carry it away with them, threw down the barricades and rushed in to drive away the watchers. On the instant they were struck blind, and transfixed as if turned to stone.

At daybreak the multitude assembled to look upon the body of Anthony and to touch it. Miracles were wrought then and there; while from time to time arose a wail from the people, who cried with one voice: "Whither have you gone, loving Father of Padua? Have you really gone away, and left behind the children who repented and were born again to Christ through you? Where shall we find another to preach to us orphans with such patience and charity?"

Owing to the non-arrival of the provincial, Brother Leo Valvasari, a very wise and prudent man—later Archbishop of Milan,—went out to calm the passions of the ever-increasing throngs. Addressing the men of Arcella, he said:

"My brothers, there can be no question of justice as regards your claim; but if you wish to retain the body of Father Anthony, asking it as a favor, I and my brethren will consult as to what seems to be the will of God. Meanwhile I gladly give you permission to watch the place where our holy Father Anthony lies, in order that you may not distrust us."

A body of armed men was sent from Padua to protect the convent of the Poor

Clares, and an order issued that any one molesting the friars, or found carrying weapons at Arcella, should be fined a hundred pounds of silver.

When the bishop held court a few days later, he summoned the Friars Minor, as well as the representatives of Capodiponte, in order that he might hear and judge both sides of the question. It was now the belated provincial who arose and said:

"Justice is a holy thing, and must never be made the sport of passion. Love and attachment are praiseworthy, but they must give way to justice. This present affair has been conducted with blind passion rather than according to the rules of justice. Who can doubt that Brother Anthony belonged to us? You all witnessed his arrival at Santa Maria; how he went in and out amongst us; how if he went on a journey it was to us he returned. A month ago he left us; but only, as he himself said, to come back in a short time, and then to remain with us altogether. I, therefore, who, although unworthy, govern this province, declare frankly Brother Anthony belongs to us, as he himself wished. We do not demand this; but we, in all humility, ask the venerated chief pastor, the honorable council, and the faithful people of Padua, to grant our petition."

The petition was granted: the Sisters of Arcella graciously resigned their claim; peace was restored; and on the 18th of June, 1231—five days after his death—the body of Anthony was solemnly conveyed from the convent of the Poor Clares to the Church of Santa Maria, in Padua. It was a triumphal procession, participated in by the bishop, the clergy, the members of the University, the civil authorities, and vast throngs of the inhabitants. The noblest of the Padovani in turn carried the bier; a myriad flaming candles borne after it were as a wake of fire.

Pontifical Mass was celebrated by the bishop; and, after the customary rites, the body was laid in a marble sarcophagus supported by four columns. From this shrine a flood of miraculous power issued. The blind saw, the deaf heard, the maimed walked, and the sick were healed. Even those who could not enter the church for the throngs that filled it to suffocation were cured in the presence of the multitudes without.

Toward the end of his life, by reason of his prolonged vigils, his continuous fasting, his arduous and unceasing labors, Anthony's form was wasted, his face haggard, his skin like drawn parchment; he was enfeebled to the verge of decrepitude. Those who looked upon his body after death found it restored to the incomparable beauty of youth. The smile of infancy played upon those fair features; a delicate flush suffused them; the limbs were once more softly rounded, and were pliable to the very last, as if he were but dreaming a sweet dream of rest. There he lay, wrapped in the innocent slumber of a child, fragrant as a dew-drenched rose — a very lily of purity plucked in its perfect prime.

XXI.—THE SORROWS OF ANTHONY.

How can a saint be sorrowful? Should not his sanctity alone be sufficient to fill him with inexpressible joy? He can sorrow for the sins of others, though he himself is sinless. Anthony no doubt did this again and again, and yet again. He can despise himself and his works, they both fall so far short of his ideal; and surely this is sorrow enough for one soul to suffer. Anthony sorrowed in like manner; but I believe this was not his chief sorrow. The source of his sorrow lay elsewhere.

In looking back through the brief history of his career, we find that, in a certain sense, Anthony's life was a series of disappointments,—was, in fact, one long disappointment from beginning to end. He did not pride himself upon his noble blood. He despised the riches that were in store for him and turned from them with contempt. He took no pleasure in the pastimes of his playmates. He sought only solitude; for his soul was ever solitary, and would fain fly away into the wilderness and there make its home.

Having found a solitude which seemed suitable in all respects, his spiritual tranquillity was disturbed by the advent of the friars who were even then far on the royal road to martyrdom. Then solitude lost its charms; he also yearned for the baptism of blood—the blessed pangs, the purifying flames, and the martyr's glorious palm. Yet these were not for him. At the very threshold of the arena, where torture and cruel death awaited their innocent victims, he was denied admittance and laid low with a fever that compelled his reluctant retreat. Here was sorrow upon sorrow; for he had been thus rudely awakened from the loftiest dream of his life.

Again his heart sought retirement, and, like the stricken deer, fled from the herd in anguish and dismay. The world he loathed with a righteous loathing; and to escape from it he feigned a simplicity of mind that, had it been genuine, must have unfitted him for almost every walk in life. Through this innocent ruse he was once more enabled to taste the sweets of solitude. There he enriched himself with those spiritual riches which he was anon to scatter broadcast through the world

Not long could he hide his light under a bushel, let him try never so hard. The breadth and beauty of his mind, the loving kindness of his heart, the splendor of his talents, the wisdom of his judgment, the depth of his penetration, the profundity of his speculations, and the luminous exposition of every theme he touched upon. nally swept him into the very vortex of political and religious contention.

This was the end of all his cherished hopes and fond aspirations. Real solitude he could never again know, save at long intervals and for a little moment; and even then he must have accused himself of leaving worldly duties unperformed for the holier and purer joy of silence and seclusion.

But sorrow's crown of sorrow awaited him. Finding himself suddenly called to his reward, with but a few hours between him and the grave, his one desire was to reach the city he had chosen for his own, and the monastery of his brother friars, where he had hoped to end his days. Within sight of the gates of that city, within sound of the monastery bell, he was stricken down to death; and for a time it seemed as if his dust would not be permitted to lie within the sanctuary of his adoption.

Therefore I say that the sorrows of

Anthony were, in a certain sense, continuous and unceasing, — that his life was one long sorrow. He bore this grievous burden meekly and in silence, with never a murmur of complaint. We have not learned from his lips or his pen a single syllable of his sufferings, mental, spiritual, or physical; but we know full well that he was a man of sorrows and acquainted with grief.

XXII.—THE JOYS OF ANTHONY.

Sorrow is for a night; joy cometh with the morning; and joys are the more joyful by reason of the sorrows that have preceded them. Life without contrasts is like a picture without light and shade—a blank. Such a life is not worth the living.

A poet has remarked: "The joy of love is loving." This is doubtless true, and this was Anthony's chief joy: he loved his fellowmen even when he sought to shun them. It was his nature to love, even as it was his nature to seek retirement, and to strive, perhaps, to forget the object of his love; for his love for God was the ruling passion of his life. As he loved all, so he won the love of all—even the love of his enemies, who straightway became his faithful followers.

Out of the abundance of his love he worked his wonders. Like a good husbandman, he went to and fro sowing peace in the field of dissension. At his approach, bringing with him as he did an atmosphere that penetrated the hardest heart and softened it, he attuned long-standing discords; he harmonized the inharmonious home circle.

To the wife fleeing from the wrath of an enraged and unreasonable husband, he said: "Return to your own home in peace." And when she had come to her own house, a kindly welcome awaited her. To the infant whose lips had not yet framed a syllable, and whose father had unjustly accused his wife of infidelity, Anthony said: "My child, I adjure thee, in the name of the Infant God of the Manger, to declare publicly, in clear and positive terms, to whom thou owest thy existence." The child, in the arms of its mother, turned toward the accuser and pronounced distinctly these three words: "Behold my father!" Then Anthony, taking the babe and placing it in the arms of the husband, said: "Love this child for it is indeed your own. Love also your wife, who has been proved to be faithful, devoted, and worthy of your affection."

What a sermon, in a few words, on true and false love, he preached at the funeral of the Florentine notable! Anthony's text was: "Where thy treasure is there thy heart is also." Pausing suddenly, he beheld in a vision the soul of that rich man in torment. He exclaimed: "This rich man is dead and his soul is in torture! Go open his coffers and you will find his heart." The astonished relatives and friends hastened to do his bidding; and there, half buried among the gold pieces, they found the still palpitating heart of the dead Crœsus.

It was Anthony's fearless joy to bring a misguided bishop to repentance. He must have been conscious of his power to impart health to the sick, and even to breathe life into the marble lips of the dead. Daily — nay, almost hourly — he brought peace to the heart that was troubled; he dried the tears of the mourner, and planted hope in the bosom of despair. These were the joys that must have visited him daily—yea, even hourly; for daily and hourly was he scattering benedictions broadcast, even as the rain from heaven that falleth alike upon the just and the unjust.

And so he passed away from sorrows that were ended, and from earthly joys to the joys of heaven,—the joys that are without beginning and without end. He passed away beloved and bewailed by peoples and by nations, whose hearts he had touched as they had never yet been touched; whose consciences he had pricked until they had goaded their possessors into new paths, where they learned to lead nobler and braver lives; whose souls he had quickened and gathered into the fold, and saved forever and forever.

XXIII.—THE GLORIES OF ANTHONY.

Numberless are the glories of Anthony, and they are ever increasing from age to age. Pope Gregory IX., who called him "the Ark of both Testaments and the storehouse of the Sacred Scriptures," longed to honor him. Under his teaching and preaching numberless heretics had been converted, rebellious cities had been reconciled, and the miracles which were being constantly wrought through his instrumentality had created astonishing fervor throughout the land; therefore it was the wish of his Holiness to attach Anthony to the Papal court and invest him with the purple. The gentle Franciscan, remembering the replies of St. Dominic and St. Francis on a like occasion, in 1217, made answer in the words of the founder of his Order. "My Lord," said the

Seraphic Father, "my children are called Friars Minor because they hold the lowest rank in the Church. This is their post of honor. Beware of taking it from them under the pretext of raising them higher." So Anthony was permitted to return into the solitude of God, and this was one of his glories.

It was a glorious privilege Anthony enjoyed when he was permitted to fly to the rescue of his father, who was in dire distress. That father—Don Martino—was still a resident of Lisbon, still basking in the favor of the King and holding high office in the court. One day a young nobleman coming from the cathedral was seized and murdered by assassins, who threw the body into the garden of Don Martino, which was close at hand. Don Martino was arrested on suspicion and cast into prison.

To Anthony the fate of his father was

miraculously revealed. Having perfect faith in his innocence, and desiring to go at once to his rescue, Anthony asked leave of the superior of the convent of Arcella to absent himself from Padua for a little time. He was himself Provincial, and not obliged to ask leave of the Father Guardian; but he never forgot the exercise of humility, for he was meekness itself. Having obtained leave of absence, he began his weary journey, scarcely knowing when or how he was to reach its end, or whether he should arrive in time to rescue his father from impending peril. Filled with hope and perfect trust, suddenly he found himself miraculously transported to Lisbon. The trial was in progress. Anthony at once entered the courts; and, presenting himself before the judges, who were struck dumb with amazement, he begged leave to speak in defence of Don Martino. He declared his father innocent. Where were his proofs? Anthony replied: "The murdered man shall bear witness as to the truth of my testimony."

Anthony led the way to the victim's grave, followed by the wondering judges and the excited populace. He commanded that the grave be opened; and when it was opened and the body was uncovered, Anthony, addressing the dead man, charged him, in the name of God, to say whether Martino de Bouillon was his murderer. Rising in his grave-clothes to a sitting posture, resting upon one hand while the other was raised to heaven, the dead declared in a loud voice that Martino de Bouillon was guiltless. Then, turning to Anthony, he begged absolution from an excommunication under which he labored; and, when his prayer was answered, he sank back into his coffin, a corpse again. Then the bewildered judges begged the Saint to reveal the name of the murderer, and he replied: "I come to clear the innocent, not to denounce the guilty." When Anthony reappeared at Arcella, he had been absent two nights and a single day.

On another occasion Don Martino, who had the management of a considerable portion of the royal exchequer, delivered a large sum of money into the hands of his subordinates, who neglected to give him a receipt for it. Some months later, when about to render his accounts he remembered that he had no receipt for certain monies delivered; and when he asked for one, those who had received the sum denied all knowledge of the transaction. It was a plot of his enemies to ruin him. While he was standing before his audacious accusers, in despair of proving his case, Anthony appeared at his side; and, naming to his accusers the exact hour and the very place when and where they had received the money, even describing the different coins in which it had been paid, he demanded that a full receipt be at once rendered to his father; and as soon as it was done he disappeared. This is one of several instances of bilocation in the miraculous history of Anthony.

He knew the minds and the hearts of all, and spoke to many at a distance, calling them by name—he had perhaps never met them face to face. At his word they were converted, and returned to the Holy Sacraments. Said Pope Gregory IX. six hundred years ago: "The supernatural which blossoms from the tombs of the elect is a continuous proclamation of truth; for by this means God confounds the malice of heretics, confirms the truth of Catholic dogma, renews the faith that is on the point of being extinguished, leads back Christians who have erred—nay, even Jews and pagans—to the feet of Him who is the Way, the Truth, and the Life."

The famous book of the Bollandists contains nearly thirty folio pages filled with the record of pure miracles. Azevedo devotes an entire book of four chapters to some of the miracles of Anthony selected by the Bollandists as most authentic. Under the head of "Death," among the classified miracles, Azevedo names a dozen cases; in each case the dead was brought to life. Under the head of "Error" he notes numerous miraculous conversions, among them a Lutheran, a Calvinist, a Turkish lady, and an Indian prince. Under the title of "Calamity" are stories of miraculous relief brought to many and various persons. Those condemned to death were delivered, the imprisoned were set free, and all manner of diseases were healed.

It is a pretty story told of a child whose mother seeing it fall from a high window, cried to Anthony for help. When the distracted mother rushed to seek her boy, he ran smiling to her and said: "A friar caught me in his arms and placed me gently on the ground." The mother took her child to the old Franciscan church of Ara Cœli, in Rome, to return thanks; and as they entered it the little fellow, pointing to a picture, said: "See!—there is the friar who saved me!" The friar was St. Anthony of Padua.

A poor leper was being carried to the shrine of Anthony when he was met by a heartless soldier who scoffingly saluted him: "Whither art thou going, wretch? May thy leprosy come upon myself if St. Anthony succeeds in curing thee!" The leper went his way; and, while praying fervently, the Saint appeared to him and said: "Arise! Thou art whole. But seek out the soldier who mocked thee and give him the clappers; for leprosy is already devouring him." (The clappers were an instrument of warning which all lepers were obliged to carry about with them when in the streets, that people might avoid infection.) He who was a leper but a few moments before found the soldier in a wretched plight. The soldier, in his turn, repented; and, calling upon the Saint, he was straightway healed.

Many were the wells he blessed, and the waters thereof cured fevers from that hour. Indeed, so wide is the range of his miracles that one may call on him in any strait.

Perhaps the tenderest devotion of all he has awakened in the guileless heart of maidenhood. At his feet she lays her heart, and asks of him guidance in the choice of its protector. Trusting him, through him she would trust his choice for her; and thus repose in perfect confidence upon the bosom of one whose lot in life she has been sought to share in a union so dear, so delicate, so devotional, it seems indeed under the immediate patronage of the most loyal and lovable of saints.

Anthony spent the first fifteen years of his brief life in his paternal home; two years at St. Vincent's, the monastery of the Canons Regular of St. Augustin, near Lisbon; nine years at Santa Cruz, in Coimbra; and about ten and a half years in the Order of the Friars Minor. He then passed away. So prodigious were the wonders worked at his tomb and through his intercession, within six months after Anthony's death the bishop of Padua petitioned the Holy See to confer on the wonder-worker the honor of canonization. The preliminary judicial inquiries were instituted without delay; and, by an exception almost unparalleled in history, before the year was ended, on Whit-Sunday, May 30, 1232, the Sovereign Pontiff Gregory IX., then at Spoleto, solemnly pronounced the decree of canonization. In it he says:

"Having ourselves witnessed the wonderful and holy life of blessed Anthony, the great wonder-worker of the universal Church, and unwilling to withhold the honor due on earth from one whom Heaven itself has surrounded with glory, we, in virtue of the plenitude of our apostolic authority, after having duly consulted our brethren the cardinals, deem it expedient to inscribe him in the calendar of saints.''

Indescribable rejoicing followed the announcement that Anthony had been declared a saint. His mother and his two sisters, who survived him, enjoyed the extraordinary privilege of witnessing the festivities given in honor of the Saint. Every city that had known him in the flesh now especially honored him; every house or hospice or haunt that he had visited became hallowed in the eyes of his followers and a place of pious pilgrimage. At Brivé, in the south of France, pilgrimages were twice interrupted and for a long time discontinued. In 1565 the Calvinists were the cause of this interruption, and in 1793 the Revolutionists. But in 1874 Monsignor Berteaux re-established the devotion; the sons of St. Francis again took possession of the hill sanctified by the prayers of the wonder-worker; and the Bishop of Tulle, on August 3, 1874, when the Franciscans were reinstated, remarked on that joyful occasion:

"To-day I, the Bishop of this diocese, in the name of the Church, take possession again of this venerable sanctuary, this celestial hill.... This spot has heard the ardent sighs of an impassioned lover of Christ,—the mighty orator who drew his mystic lore from the Sacred Scriptures and deserved to be styled by Gregory IX. 'the Ark of the Testament.' His commentaries on the divine pages may be likened to a golden harp sending forth magnificent harmonies to the glory of the Word Incarnate. The Child Jesus Himself touched his lips and his fingers, that they might pour forth golden words. This inspired preacher of the word of God, whom we call Anthony of Padua, has trodden these valleys and plains, has prayed and watched in this lonely cave, has slaked his thirst in this clear water which is a reflection of the purity of his soul. To-day I bid you welcome, sons of St. Francis, to this spot, once inhabited by your brother, the great wonder-worker. Proclaim Christ wheresoever you go; . . . and in all your strivings imitate your holy brother in St. Francis, the great St. Anthony of Padua.''

Brivé is annually the resort of thousands of pilgrims; and not Brivé only and the valley of the Corrèze: everywhere and under many forms St. Anthony is venerated. At Vaucluse and elsewhere it has been the custom to invoke St. Anthony in order to insure a plentiful harvest. In a breviary of the fourteenth century belonging to the diocese of Apt we find the following form of blessing,—it is the blessing of the seed-grain:

"Bless, O Lord! this seed; and, through the merits of our blessed father St. Anthony, deign to multiply it, and cause it to bring forth fruit a hundredfold; and preserve it from lightning and tempest. Who livest and reignest world without end. Amen."

In the same volume is found the following prayer used when a blessing was invoked upon a child; and a measure of corn—the weight of the child—was distributed among the poor:

"We humbly beseech Thy clemency, O Lord Jesus Christ! through the merits and prayers of our most glorious father St. Anthony, that Thou wouldst deign to preserve from all ill — fits, plague, epidemic, fever and mortality — this Thy servant, who, in Thy name and in honor of our blessed father St. Anthony, we place in this balance with wheat, the weight of his body, for the comfort of the poor sick who suffer in this hospital. Deign to give him length of days, and permit him to attain the evening of life; and, by the merits and prayers of the Saint we invoke, grant him a portion in Thy holy and eternal inheritance, guarding and preserving him from all his enemies. Who livest and reignest with the Father and the Holy Ghost world without end. Amen."

XXIV.—AN UNFADING MEMORY.

From the very first, confraternities in honor of St. Anthony have existed in many parts of the world. With the revival of the spirit of Catholic devotion, the love for St. Anthony increased. His blessed name had ever been associated with the relief of the wants of the poor; and a favorite form of charity, in his name, has been the liberal bestowal of loaves among the hungry and impoverished. This bread has come to be known as the bread of St. Anthony.

Says a good woman, writing as late as 1892, from Toulon:

"I promised bread to St. Anthony for his poor if he would help me, and he *has* helped me. All my friends pray with me to the good Saint, and all our troubles are commended to him with a promise of bread to his poor. We are astonished at the graces thus obtained. One of my most intimate friends promised a certain amount of bread every day of her life if a member of her family could be cured of a fault that had caused her great grief for three and twenty years, and the prayer was granted. In thanksgiving she bought a little statue of St. Anthony, and we put it up in a dark corner where we require a big lamp to see it. And now my backshop is filled all day with people in fervent prayer. Not only do they pray, but one would think that they were paid to spread this devotion, so zealously do they do so. Sometimes a soldier, an officer, a sea-captain, going for a long voyage, will promise so much per month in bread to St. Anthony if they make their journey safely. Sometimes it is a mother asking for the health of her sick child, or perhaps for the success of an examination. Then, again, it is a family asking for the conversion of one amongst them who is dying and will not see a priest; a servant out of a place, or working people out of work; and all these petitions, which are accompanied with the promise of bread, are granted."

The Universal Association of St. Anthony of Padua, founded by Don Locatilli at the request and with the blessing of Pope Leo XIII., has been established at Padua. It now numbers nearly 260,000 members. The Pious Union—a similar organization—is flourishing in Rome. Here and there in England and Ireland, chiefly in convents, the bread-givers have given freely in St. Anthony's name.

There is a humble little Franciscan monastery church at Crawley, Sussex, England. Within that church is a chapel which for a long time was not dedicated to any special object. Recently a remarkably fine portrait of St. Anthony was discovered at Crawley; it was placed in the unoccupied chapel, and the chapel was dedicated to the Saint. Thus was established the Guild of St. Anthony; its object, the promotion of devotion to St. Anthony and to propagate the work of the distribution of his Bread to the Poor. "Masses and other spiritual advantages are given to its members, who are placed under no other obligation than the entering of their names in the register kept for that purpose at Crawley." The alms, or the bread promised in the name of St. Anthony, can be given wherever the donor pleases. Any reader who is interested in this beautiful charity can learn full particulars by applying — in person or through the mails — to the Rev. Father Guardian, O. S. F. C., Franciscan Monastery, Crawley, Sussex, England.

When faith has been at a low ebb devotion to our Saint has not dwindled. At Auges, where there is a very precious relic of St. Anthony, the inhabitants have been ever loyal to a man. A hard-working peasant is reported to have said to his son, with more enthusiasm than judgment: "You may work on Sundays and you may work on holydays—even Christmas and Easter—*if you must;* but if you are so wicked as to work on St. Anthony's Day I will hang you from the highest gable of the house."

The body of St. Anthony was brought into Padua on Tuesday. It is a well-attested fact that no single sufferer who invoked his aid on that day failed to be cured. In 1617 a lady of Bologna, who in her distress had appealed to St. Anthony, saw in a dream his likeness. The Saint opened his lips and said: "Go on nine consecutive Tuesdays and visit the chapel of the Friars Minor; there receive Holy Communion, and thy prayers shall be granted." And it was as he had promised her. This miracle gave rise to the devotion of the Nine Tuesdays in honor of St. Anthony; later it was increased to thirteen, in honor of the date of his death.

For more than thirty years the body of the Saint remained in its marble shrine in the Church of Santa Maria Maggiore; but the friars and the people were not content, and in 1263 it was translated by St. Bonaventure to the high altar of a new church built by the Friars Minor in his honor. On opening the shrine at this time, it was found that the body had returned to dust, but the tongue was incorrupt and of a natural color. St. Bonaventure exclaimed in a transport of devotion: "O blessed tongue, which always didst bless the Lord and cause others to bless Him, now does it appear plainly how highly thou wert esteemed by God!"

In 1310 his body was again translated to a chapel which had been built expressly for it. This chapel did not satisfy the devotion of the friars; and still another, far more commodious and splendid, was erected, and thither the remains were translated in 1350. Many relics had been scattered among churches in various parts of Europe; and these were, as far as possible, gathered together, and in 1745 they were all solemnly deposited in the magnificent receptacle where they are now venerated.

In 1749 the church was nearly destroyed by fire, yet the altar of the Saint was quite uninjured. While the flames were raging fiercely, crowds of people were seen climbing upon the sagging roof and hurrying through the building in the midst of smoke and falling timbers; and, though many fell among the glowing coals and were struck by flying firebrands, no one was injured.

The church and the chapel are among the richest and most beautiful in the world, and these alone are sufficient to attract thousands annually to Padua. His is the ruling spirit there; one thinks only of him. Often a hideous little carving of bone or wood or metal is offered you for a mere trifle; and his medals, his photographs, copies of portaits of surpassing loveliness, are for sale on every street corner. Within that shrine what splendor delights the eye! All that can be done with marble and bronze, and silver and gold and precious stones has been superbly done in the ornamentation of that wondrous mausoleum.

Three sunburnt fishermen were kneeling with their foreheads resting on the sculptured marble of the tomb when I last drew near it. Is not good San Antonio the protector of all seafarers? Do not fair winds come through his intercession? Are not his medals and statuettes worn by devout Christian sailors the wide seas over?

Having spent hours of rare refreshment in that glorious temple, and gathered my little store of pious objects, I returned to mine inn for rest. From the windows I saw the lofty walls of Il Santo—the Basilica of

San Antonio—towering against the sunset. There is nothing finer than the proportions of this wondrous structure. Larger than San Marco at Venice, it is far more impressive when viewed from without. There are a hundred gables that toss like a broken sea. Clusters of delicate spires spring into space like frozen fountains; and over all rise seven splendid domes that seem to be floating in mid-air. One almost fears that the whole will melt away in the twilight, and leave only the spot that it once glorified—like an Arabian tale that is told. Surely its creation was magical. Some *genie*, sporting with the elements, made marble soluble; and, dreaming of the fabulous East, he blew this pyramid of gigantic bubbles, and had not the heart to let them break and vanish. Or is it but another miracle of the beloved Saint?

St. Anthony of Padua has been hailed as the Eminent Doctor, the defender of the

Divinity of the Incarnate Word, and the vindicator of the Real Presence. He was also the champion and the apostle of the glorious mystery of Mary's Assumption, as the Patriarch of Assisi had been of her Immaculate Conception. It was St. Anthony who uttered the versicle incorporated in her Office on the Assumption: "The august Mother of God has been assumed into heaven and placed above the angelic choirs." What proof had he of this? Our Blessed Lady appeared to him; with his eyes he saw her in her glory; with enraptured ears he listened to her voice celestial as she said: "Be assured, my son, that this my body, which has been the living ark of the Word Incarnate, has been preserved from the corruption of the grave. Be equally assured that, three days after my death, it was carried upon the wings of angels to the right hand of the Son of God, where I reign Queen."

Therefore, with a heart filled with indescribable joy, he exclaimed: "The Virgin of Nazareth has, by a singular privilege, been preserved from the original stain and filled with a plenitude of grace. Hail, O Mother of God, city of refuge, sublime mountain, throne of the Most High, fruitful vine yielding golden grapes, flooding the hearts of men with the holy exaltation of pure love! Hail, Star of the Sea! Thy gentle and radiant light is our guide in the darkness, showing us the entrance to the harbor above. Woe to the pilot whose eyes are not fixed on thee! His frail bark will become the plaything of the storm, and will be swallowed up in the foaming billows."

The glowing tributes which have been paid to St. Anthony of Padua would fill volumes, yet the noblest tribute of all is the silent but ardent love his millions of followers have given him. Nothing need be added to this, yet I will add what St.

Bonaventure said: that St. Anthony was "an angelic soul," and that his crown of glory was enriched with all the gems of grace and perfection distributed amongst the other saints. "He possessed the science of the angels, the faith of the patriarchs, the foreknowledge of the prophets, the zeal of the apostles, the purity of virgins, the austerities of confessors, and the heroism of martyrs."

St. Antoninus, the illustrious Archbishop of Florence, says of St. Anthony: "He was a vessel of election, an eagle in knowledge, a wonder-worker beyond compare." And the Franciscan Liturgy adds: "A violet of humility, a lily of chastity, a rose of divine charity." He was the ardent advocate, the favorite and the champion of the Sacred Heart. Three centuries after his death the Venerable Jane Mary of the Cross describes the following vision with which she was blessed:

"While in prayer on the Feast of St. Anthony, I saw the soul of this Saint borne by angels to the feet of Christ. Our Lord opened wide the wound of His Heart; and this Heart, all radiant with light, attracted and seemed, in some sort, to absorb the soul of St. Anthony, as the light of the sun absorbs all other light. In the Heart of Jesus the soul of the Saint appeared to me like a precious gem of radiating brilliancy, which filled all the cavity. The varied play of its colors represented to me the virtues of the Saint. They shone with marvellous splendor in the ocean of light proceeding from the Heart of Jesus, to the honor of Christ and the glory of the Saint himself. Then Jesus took this lustrous gem in His Heart and presented it to His Heavenly Father, who caused it to be admired by the angels and saints."

. . . . . .

"When you hear that I am a saint, then

bless ye the Lord." These words, that fell from the lips of the youthful Anthony when he first went in search of martyrdom, were not addressed to his brethren at the Abbey of Santa Cruz alone: they are as fresh and as appealing now as they ever were; they are alive and shall always remain alive; and to-day—now—this very hour—they are addressed to me and to you, and to everyone that lives or shall live in ages to come, even unto the end of the world.

"Bless ye the Lord!"

www.ingramcontent.com/pod-product-compliance
Lightning Source LLC
Chambersburg PA
CBHW020241170426
43202CB00008B/173